WHY COME BACK?

BOOK 2

WHY COME BACK? BOOK 2

FURTHER SPIRITUAL INSIGHTS INTO WHY YOU ARE HERE

ROGER J BURMAN

Quiet Waters Publishing Ltd

First published in 2002

Copyright © 2002 Roger J Burman

This book is copyrighted under the Berne Convention. No portion may be reproduced by any process without the copyright holder's written permission except for the purpose of reviewing or criticism, as permitted under the Copyright Act of **1956**.

British Library Cataloguing in Publication Data

A catalogue record for this book is available from the British Library

ISBN 0-9542047-1-9

Typeset by CityScape Books
www.cityscapebooks.co.uk

Published by Quiet Waters Publishing Ltd
North Lodge, The Pines, Boston Road
Sleaford, Lincolnshire NG34 7DN
www.quiet-waters.net

Printed and bound in Great Britain
By Antony Rowe, Eastbourne

CONTENTS

7   INTRODUCTION

19 CHAPTER ONE – Our past lives as a case study

40 CHAPTER TWO – Further case study past lives

55 CHAPTER THREE – Discussion on case study; Soul Groups; Freewill

70 CHAPTER FOUR – Our current lives under the microscope

89 CHAPTER FIVE – Spiritual letters

101 CHAPTER SIX – Past life mediumship case studies, Eva and Cheryl

128 CHAPTER SEVEN – Contact with spirit; Ghosts; Mediumship; Alternative Therapies; Fairies; Self Healing; More about guides

153 CHAPTER EIGHT – More from the mediumship case book

175 CHAPTER NINE – More about the spirit world; Spirit Council; Council of Elders; Soul Study Groups; Spirit and time; The future known; Conclusion

193 APPENDIX ONE – More about animal spirits

198 APPENDIX TWO – Dealing with scepticism

206 BIBLIOGRAPHY

"Our revels now are ended. These our actors,
As I foretold you, were all spirits and
Are melted into air, into thin air:
And, like the baseless fabric of this vision,
The cloud-capped towers, the gorgeous palaces,
The Solemn temples, the great globe itself,
Yea, all which it inherit, shall dissolve
And, like this insubstantial pageant faded,
Leave not a rack behind. We are such stuff
As dreams are made on, and our little life
Is rounded with a sleep.

Shakespeare, *The Tempest*

INTRODUCTION

It is the way of an incarnation into a nursery world that one arrives without knowledge (in the main) of the reasons for being there and without knowledge of the spirit that one is.

I liken this to a player in a team game, football, rugby or similar. The player finds himself on the pitch, wearing the appropriate kit, with spectators in the background. Suddenly he suffers complete amnesia. He wonders how he came to be in the stadium, what the other people are doing and what he is supposed to do. He tries his hardest to search his memory for clues. Nothing! He stares inquisitively at the other players; no response! He looks around, but cannot find a notice board with instructions. Suddenly the ball hits him causing a sharp pain. People rush by, shouting incoherently. The shock and disorientation causes paralysis.

This is one metaphor for our birth on planet Earth, the nursery world of incarnation. We arrive here without a rulebook and need to work out the rules to unblock our paralysis. Many will not make the attempt; the majority that choose to incarnate on Earth are younger spirits, and for them the accepted views, the norms of the society will be adopted and they will become crowd members, living out conventional lives. This is as intended, for them growth will be achieved late in the incarnation, or even on return to spirit.

For some, a much smaller number of older spirits, those that have achieved a higher degree of spiritual awareness prior to incarnation, this will not be sufficient. They will seek the meaning of life, bring into question the accepted ways and go on a spiritual quest. To those persons, this book is particularly addressed. For these higher evolved spirits, the challenge of being incarnated into this world of little spirituality without knowledge of one's spiritual self is great. The huge potential to climb out of a state of ignorance and achieve spiritual progression is not provided for other than on a nursery world.

MY STORY:

I have been attempting to climb up the ladder of knowledge since my teenage years, but did not find the spiritual staircase until my mid-forties, as was intended in my particular life-plan. I started as many do, by visiting a medium, following the death of my mother, who died from a debilitating illness at a young age.

Later I lost my only brother through a tragic accident. At the same time as his death in 1995, I suffered the collapse of my marriage and forced separation from my children as the result of the traumatic divorce that followed. My quest for the meaning of such a waste of life, and such trauma, led me from my initial contact with a medium, to begin an avid search to know more. Why must we suffer? Is it bad luck, is it karma, or maybe a punishing deity?

I am sure this sounds like a familiar pathway for many. I read voraciously, consuming books about mediumship, alternative beliefs, spiritual and psychic matters, reincarnation, the afterlife and so on, with a growing hunger. I discovered and was enraptured by the *"Conversations with God"* books by Neale Donald Walsch; I attended spiritual churches, development circles and "special" events; I had my aura photographed. Eventually, I underwent a past life regression which proved the consolidating factor in my belief in reincarnation.

Having confirmed such a belief, the next logical question for me was why? If as I now believed, we are all spiritual beings having an earthly experience and we apparently repeat this experience several times, why? If life can be this cruel, why come back? I found myself a girlfriend, who initially shared my interest in spiritual matters, but by the end of 1999 her interest had waned and this together with other factors, led to the end of the relationship as the century drew to an end too. By this time, I had arrived at an unshakeable belief in the continuance of spirit and a belief in reincarnation and was now unsure where to go next with my quest. Early in the new millennium, January 2000 to be exact, I met Angie!

ANGIE'S STORY:

Angie has been spiritually aware from childhood, in fact, for as long as she can remember. She was as she puts it, "fortunate in her maternal grandmother", who partially raised her. This grandmother was herself extremely spiritual and psychic, and so as a child, her gift received, at least from that quarter, the nurturing it required.

Her grandmother taught her to keep her ability to herself and not to speak of it to other children who may ridicule her for it, or to adults who would try to suppress it and treat it as over-active imagination. Remember, this was the 1950s in rural England. They had ceased to burn witches at the stake, but probably only just! (Just joking!)

This grandmother taught her how to use her gift and how to communicate with spirit as easily as she did with people; easier in fact, as she was a shy and self-conscious only child, more comfortable with adults than her contemporaries. Her grandmother recognised that the ability the child had was extremely developed, more so even than her own, and wished to guard it.

In Angie's early teens, this development came to an abrupt halt however, following the death of her grandmother. It remained dormant, with only occasional flare-ups, until a severe car accident in the early 1980s broke her spine, among other things, and left her severely disabled. In daily agonising pain and unable to walk properly, she eventually sought the assistance of a spiritual healer, all else having apparently failed.

This healer recognised her spirituality and asked her which church she attended or what form her mediumship took. He was amazed to find that she was not working spiritually in any way, and persuaded her to go with him to his church. Together they worked on her pain and disability, and to the great amazement of the assorted medical professionals responsible for her care, she improved. She still has some problems relating to the incident, but is mended to a degree never envisaged. She now walks again, even climbs ladders occasionally, whereas once the prognosis was wheelchair bound for life.

More importantly to her, immediately she attended the church with her healer, she felt that she had "come home"; all her previously held abilities came flooding back, together with many new ones. She found herself accurately able to give tarot readings, do psychometry, see and interpret aura, give spiritual communication on an individual basis, and most incredible to her, do deep trance mediumship, giving channelled philosophy and teaching to a small group. She never attempted platform mediumship due to her natural shyness.

In 1995, exactly the same year as I, she suffered a traumatic divorce. This brought her group participation to an end, even though her spiritual communication did not leave her. She was hurt and angry and tried to shut out her guide, but without too much success. She was determined to remain alone for the rest of her days, having no wish to allow another man into her life in case doing so exposed her to hurt again. She upheld this decision until Christmas 1999, when she found circumstances conspiring to make her rethink her situation. She began to think that maybe a male friend to share celebrations with and the odd outing might not be such a bad idea. After all she reasoned, she could keep a distance between them. Then in January 2000 she met me!

THE STORY FROM JANUARY 2000:

THE FIRST BOOK, *"WHY COME BACK?"*

Talk about a meeting of minds! We quickly realised that there was more to this meeting than met the eye. Our individual spirituality increased in leaps and bounds over a matter of months. We experienced a telepathy between us, greater than any we had known before. Angie found herself "pushed" by her guide to relay information to me. I found I could ask questions and receive answers straight from spirit; I had found the source of the answers I had been searching for since my spiritual awakening, indeed since my early questions about the meaning of life as a teenager.

So began a year of channelled information. Every question I asked was answered, some with a few lines, some with pages and pages. Angie found that her preferred means of communicating the information was to write it down, rather like taking dictation. This she found was less open to misinterpretation by her. Her writing was such scrawl in her haste to get the information down as she received it, that it was practicably illegible, so this led to her typing the information out so I could read it.

This quickly changed to typing the information direct onto her laptop computer, spirit communication 21st century style!! It kept coming, pages of it, and eventually we were told it was the content of a book I was to write, this being the first of several books.

The information received forms the content of my first book, *"Why Come Back? A Spiritual Insight Into Why You Are Here"*. It explains for those that have an acceptance of past lives, the purpose of the many incarnations of the soul. It explains how the concepts of *"you are here for experience"* and *"you are here to learn about love"* are achieved through each one of us having a life-plan and what goes into it.

It does not conform in some cases with the opinions supported by spiritual organisations. It contradicts, or rather corrects, some of the beliefs held about the working of spirit and the means of spiritual communication, but more importantly, it introduces a whole new piece of information, a piece of the puzzle that makes sense of so much, the concept of spiritual Threes.

Angela, our guide and myself are an example of a spiritual Three. She and I are the incarnated two thirds, while our other third remains in spirit this time as guide to the two of us. We have all shared lives on countless occasions, two incarnating and the one remaining behind, acting as guide to the other two. This is the same for every incarnated being, each is part of a three, and will have an incarnated third enter their life at some time, be it as parent, sibling, teacher, partner, friend or enemy. A third is not always a catalyst for good in one's life. The third is the true meaning of "soul mate", a term to which we popularly attribute romantic attachment. The two incarnated thirds will always meet at some point, and will often have a life-changing impact on each other. Our own meeting is an example of this, as subsequently both our lives have radically changed direction.

We are told that the introduction of this new information forms part of a natural progression for mankind's spiritual awareness; that information is drip-fed by spirit as they feel we as a race, are ready for it. Each writer and each channel of spiritual information leads on from previous ones in much the same way as the natural evolution of thinking and scientific fact now proves that the world is round not flat and is quite definitely not the centre of the universe. As little as a few hundred years ago men died for daring to hold such a contrary belief, an illustration of the difficult and arid soil new facts sometimes have to suffer before gaining germination.

PAST LIFE MEDIUMSHIP

Early in our relationship, I relayed the story of my past life regression. I wished that I could have known more about the life, which was a First World War experience. Immediately Angie's guide provided detailed information, including name, means and date of death, details of family and so on. He and I had incarnated into that life, leaving the spirit that is now Angie to act as our guide. I had also received pictures of a second life during the regression, one, it transpired, that I had shared with Angie, and he filled in the missing information about it too.

This opened up a new facet to Angie's mediumship, and since then we have together given detailed information including researchable dates, names, events and the like, to a growing group of people. The word kept spreading and the circle of people we were able to do this for widened.

How we conduct a sitting of past life mediumship is that the enquirer provides details of their likes and dislikes, fears and phobias, persons, places and things they are attracted to or repelled by, hobbies and interests etc, and Angie provides, if there exists, the past life reason for much of it.

Some have found it a deeply moving experience and have been helped greatly by it; some just find it immensely interesting. In some cases it has explained and alleviated deep held phobias without either the need to succumb to hypnosis or the trauma some associate with regression. The therapeutic value still seems to be effective without the need for the enquirer to personally experience the incident as they would in a regression.

Each enquirer leaves with Angie's trademark typescript of the session, as she continues to type what she hears rather than give it verbally. My role is to fill in the resulting conversation gaps. If the particular enquirer has such an interest, I do this either with information and teaching on the philosophy which forms the content of my books or with cups of tea and general spiritual chat if not. My degree work in psychology helps greatly here, too.

Although Angie has given this service solo on occasion, she finds my presence at the session invaluable, as I act as a kind of battery boost to her, enabling her to work for longer and with more clarity. Angie does not feel comfortable giving spiritual messages from deceased loved ones; she feels there are mediums that are destined to do this work, but that it is not really her forte. However, in a few cases, where the enquirer has experienced a loss with which they have not yet come to terms, she has found herself persuaded by the spirit guides to relay such messages. This communication has taken the form of a dictated letter from the spirit concerned direct to the bereaved person.

These letters have been gladly and gratefully (and tearfully) received, and carry unmistakable proof of the continuance of the loved one in spirit. They have answered questions left unanswered, laid to rest carried hurt or grievance and explained much. In some cases an answering letter has been transmitted from the bereaved back to spirit and a few lines of confirmation received, sufficient for it to be known that it has been received and acknowledged. Despite this, her role, she feels, is as a past life medium and a channel of spiritual philosophy for me to interpret and write into books only.

OUR CREDENTIALS

Our credentials are simply a desire to serve and work for the spiritual progression of others, and indeed ourselves. We both believe that spiritualism should not be beset with rules and regulations; that no hierarchy, such as those that control orthodox religions, should govern it.

We do not believe that any incarnated beings should feel themselves sufficiently superior to set rules for spirit to abide by. Because of this, we do not seek to be registered with any spiritual organising body. We do not feel such a registration makes the quality of spiritual communication any better or more worthy. In fact, there are cases where such organisations could be said to feed the human trait of one-upmanship.

By this, we do not intend to decry the excellent mediums that may have sought registration as a means of identifying themselves as genuine; to set themselves apart from those that seek to exploit for purely monetary gain. We just believe that such registration is not for us. Rather, we think it is important that genuine mediumship can be accepted in whatever form it presents itself, without the need for a registration to validate it. We believe that if a communication is genuine and given with love and for the progress of mankind, it should not be stopped or disbelieved because the deliverer of the information is not working in some accepted method or registered by some controlling authority.

We are told that we are not beginners at the game of life; in fact we are told, we are probably heading for retirement soon! This will most probably be apparent from the past life details we reveal. As older spirits, we are tasked with the bringing of new information to our place of incarnation. The details we give of spiritual Threes and their workings, are examples of this new information. In this instance, our place of incarnation is of course, planet Earth, the nursery world for spirit. The challenges and difficulties found here are unique, which is why older spirit chose it.

An historical parallel to us of one who was tasked with the introduction of new information, was Nostradamus, who at the time of his incarnation, was trying to complete a life-plan to teach and bring enlightenment to his time. As we know, this revolved around his own prophecies, which were possible because of his detailed knowledge of the plan for the planet. The prophecies were given as catalysts for spiritual growth, but unfortunately were not interpreted that way by the majority.

The reader may be aware of predictions that our world would end in the year 2000. Nostradamus among others made this claim. What they actually saw was the end of the Earth's cycle, not the Earth itself. Our planet has spiritual cycles of 2000 years each. One of these is just coming to a close and another is beginning. This is the reason for the phenomenon of new information being supplied; it is also the reason for a period of "catch up" our race has been undergoing. (To explain, if one looks at human history, one can see spurts in technological advances, most noticeably more recently.)

As the end of a cycle is reached, it is necessary to make sure that all that should be accomplished in that span has been accomplished, much like the end of a semester in a school. In order to achieve the required syllabus, spirit of certain ability has reincarnated on Earth to help with the "catch up". This will continue for some time in order that the new cycle starts off well. In the next cycle, is the time for our planet to take a spiritual leap. The new spiritual knowledge being sent to Earth, the incarnation of more masters than usual, the increasing number of children returning with memory of past lives and spirit life are all in preparation for the next cycle.

THE SECOND BOOK

This is intended to build on the first, in which I gave an outline of the spiritual journey and the reasoning behind major events in life. In chapters one and two, I now consider these in far greater detail, by using our own past lives as a case study. Let me say here, before anyone should think it, that I do not use my own current and past lives at length in this book for any ego serving reasons, but purely as a means of illustration of life-plan and the spiritual lessons we may be intended to learn from major life events.

I use the events from lives of others that have sought mediumship from us, too, with of course, the names changed to protect anonymity. A spirit guide respects a code of confidentiality, and will only discuss events in a life, with the specific enquirer of the life concerned, or one who is directly affected by the events in that life. Therefore the lives I was able to ask the most questions about, and so receive the most insight into, were my own.

My guide relayed detailed information concerning the events in both my current and past lives; the information was given to me in such detail, he advised, for the purpose of illustrating the spiritual teachings I was receiving and was required to pass on in my books only. (If I am completely honest, I did sneak in a question or two to satisfy my own curiosity, but of course, he would know that, too, being privy, as are all spirit guides, to my innermost thoughts. Quite a sobering concept!)

The subject of chapters one and two is therefore my past lives, and the intended reasons for the events in them, which I hope will have a fascination for the reader. Believe me, we all have past lives and they will in most cases, be as varied as my own. The actual numbers will not be the same. I believe mine to be relatively low at fourteen lives on Earth (this is not the total number of my lives of course, as only a proportion of lives are spent here). Sylvia Browne, the well-known American past life therapist, for example, admits to fifty-four lives here on Earth.

Having returned to human form fourteen times, it would be worthwhile to summarise the reasons why, which I do at the start of chapter three. I then recount the discussion I had with our guide on two of these lives and on some spiritual topics in general.

Not in a month of quiet contemplation, would I have arrived at the real reasons for the major events in my life to date, certainly not in the amount of detailed explanation I relate in chapter four. Although this is about my life, the events themselves are not unique to me, of course. New insights are offered to any reader with similar experiences.

Chapter five contains the spiritual letters that I referred to earlier. I find these deeply moving. The written page cannot, of course, relay the emotions that were felt in their giving and receiving of these letters.

For those newly on the path of spiritual search, the past life clues I list in chapter six will hopefully bolster their beliefs. The evidence is around us, we just need to recognise its true nature and not be dismissive. Unfortunately, our upbringing, culture and society are largely all against us, but change is happening, especially with the arrival of the new millennium.

Chapter seven contains more of the philosophy and teaching points that arose from the mediumship for past life enquiries and also from my own questioning of spirit. It covers a miscellany of topics, including different forms of contact with spirit and more about spirit guides.

There have been numerous occasions in past life mediumship, the subject of chapter eight, when the enquirer has felt strong emotions. This has occurred when hearing the details of a life that they then "remember", but most frequently, upon properly meeting their guide. In some instances an enquirer has been able to visualise as well as feel the presence of their guide, when

Angela gave the name and description and introduced them. This chapter would not be possible without the various enquirers for mediumship, whom we thank for the related teachings they have provided. These put "the human experience" into the spiritual perspective by discussing many major life-events. I hope the reader agrees with me that this is perhaps the most fascinating chapter of the book.

Chapter nine discusses Spirit Council and a number of aspects of the spiritual dimension. I regret I have not covered all of the topics I promised in book one; the remainder will be covered in a further book.

I have more details to give about animal spirits. As this topic is not directly concerned with why we return to human form, I have included it as appendix one.

Appendix two deals with the scepticism that surrounds spiritual beliefs; why some, men in particular, have difficulty with acceptance and what best to do in the quest for inner peace.

It is my great privilege to present this channelled information to you.

Roger Burman
Quiet Waters
Northumbria
2002

CHAPTER ONE

PAST LIFE MEDIUMSHIP

OUR PAST LIVES AS A CASE STUDY

There are, I believe, only a comparatively small number of persons fortunate enough to have, whilst incarnated, knowledge of all their past lives on Earth. Angela and I are lucky enough to be within that number. The details were not given for our own gratification, but as examples of the spiritual journey. I have therefore, no ego motive in laying before you my spiritual biography; I use my past lives purely as a case study. Although I have one past life that is documented, that of a sea captain, the remainder are, as one might expect, quite ordinary.

Indeed, for the numerous enquirers for whom my partner Angela has given past life mediumship, their past lives have been similarly "ordinary". At the time of writing, the only exceptions are one enquirer who had a past life as the French composer Francois Couperin in the seventeenth century, a life that is documented in specialist music books; one who had a past life as Molière, a French playwright also of the seventeenth century, and three others who had a distant family connection to King Richard III of England. Interestingly, they have connections in this life too. We have also encountered a Victoria Cross holder, an officer from the Gordon Highlanders, who won his medal in the second Afghan War in 1879.

In the cynics view, so many claim a famous life, Napoleon, Cleopatra and so on, that they cannot all be true. How does one overcome disbelief? In everyday life, there are many clues to past lives. One of these may be a feeling of closeness or familiarity with certain friends or family members, which defies a rational explanation. Sometimes this feeling of familiarity can extend to knowing the others thoughts without them being voiced. I believe it true to say psychology, the science of human behaviour, would not be able to explain for example, this feeling of familiarity with a comparative stranger.

I can give two personal illustrations, which have a past life explanation. When my partner Angela met her friend Ann through their respective young children, they virtually exchanged life stories at the first meeting. This was totally out of character, for both of them are quite private people; it was as if they were catching up on each other's news. Unbeknown to them at the time, this was exactly what they were doing, as they had been friends in a previous life in Ancient Egypt.

A similar incident happened in the case of Angela's second son of her marriage. Early in our relationship he came to 'vet' me as a suitable boyfriend for his mother, with a negative frame of mind. He surprised himself to find he quite liked me and could find nothing negative to say or warn his mother about. We recently learned through his having past life mediumship that he was our joint son in a past life in Elizabethan England.

The best evidence is obviously the first hand type, of memories within the soul. Many people have now experienced glimpses of past lives in individual or group special events held with that purpose in mind. Access to past life memories, those recalled in therapy for example, are not under the individual's sole control as it is the enquirer's spirit guide who controls access to them. Only those memories required at that time will be allowed to surface. The guide monitors and filters all communication and all past life information, both that delivered by the method Angela uses and that delivered direct to the enquirer by way of therapy, hypnosis or relaxation technique. Those who "get nothing" by either means are not ready to receive any information and so the guide delivers nothing.

Past life memory of non-earth lives is even more controlled, our guide advised. Only those ready to accept this type of information will be allowed access to it by the guides. Those who receive it and have difficulty with it are ready to receive it, or their guide would not have allowed it to be given to them. It is likely that part of the task for this life is for them to work through the difficulty. At the time of writing, we have only met one person who has actual memory of a non-earth past life.

To have the memory without the need to undergo a regression experience, is even more compelling evidence. We have met only one person so far, with spontaneous past life recall. He would visit certain places in the world and have flashbacks to a previous period. For example, he went to a Roman amphitheatre in what is now Libya. In the flashback, he saw the theatre full of people, heard the crowd. In mediumship, Angela confirmed he had lived several times in the Roman era, and described those and other lives to him.

The evidence sometimes comes through a tortuous route. Some people have a medical condition not subject to a ready diagnosis, often labelled "psychosomatic". I have heard a past life therapist say that she is often consulted as a last resort, when all conventional methods have been tried and failed. This seems to contain a spiritual teaching point, in that the seeking of such an unconventional treatment is part of the life-plan to become more spiritually aware. Our guide confirmed this, linking it with my own life for the point of illustration. He answered my question as follows (Angela is referred to as sister):

"Everything that happens within a lifetime is for the singular purpose of the soul's progression and awareness. As you know, for some this awareness can come as late as on the death bed, or even not at all in the incarnation, but in the review on return to spirit.

We have covered the points about the varying traumas in lives and the spiritual lessons learned. Indeed, in your own incarnation this time and that of our sister, your mutual growth has been fostered by the traumas you have experienced, which, particularly in your own case, were instrumental in precipitating your spiritual quest. The traumas in your life led you to seek out answers from mediums, led you to a spiritual church, and eventually to recognise and be attracted by the spirituality of your other third, our sister, and to have the opportunity of fulfilling your spiritual plan for this life, of achieving your destiny.

Given the above scenario, it is easy to see that a trauma that leads one to seek past life therapy is actually the first stepping stone for many to a belief in the continuance of life, a belief in the spiritual dimension, acceptance of past lives and more.

True, not all those who seek this therapy continue to progress spiritually when the therapy has done its work, but a great many do. It is quite a profound experience for many, and comes as near to "proof" as one is likely to come in the incarnated state. Those who do not use the experience as a springboard for their own progression whilst incarnated, learn from the experience on return to spirit and so again, it can be a major part of their plan in this way."

My personal comment here is that for anyone requiring proof or corroboration, then there are many books now published by past life therapists of their case files. The hardened sceptics no doubt, would actually need to have their own personal evidence, which they would be unlikely to seek. It should be borne in mind, that not everyone's life-plan is written with the intention of reaching full spiritual awareness. For the "half-sceptical", sufficient "evidence" may be obtained by coming into contact with those who have had spiritual experiences, hearing for example of others who have been dismissive of the whole idea of spirit up to the moment when they have a spiritual encounter or experience.

We have come to realise that the purpose of receiving past life information is not just the thrill of realising you had actual experience of historical facts or that you were a person of note, but the lessons that were learned in the incarnation, the spiritual progression gained or not gained. These are discussed in some detail in our own case, more so that we have been able to do for other enquirers.

True, it is fun to realise that we were noted in history or that we actually experienced something that we thought we had only read about. Our guide advised that the fun should always remain, as it is the fun that will bring many to seek the information in the first instance, and he asked us not be dismissive of it. He went on to say that moving on from the fun would be the enlightenment for some. For others it will always just be fun in this life, but will possibly be an aid to their level of development in that it awakens acceptance of reincarnation, the first step!

TIMELINE

We have produced a "timeline" of our past lives on Earth, which is reproduced at the end of chapter two. This might be constructed for all enquiring persons, except to say it is quite time-consuming and demanding on Angela, to give such an amount of information from one's spirit guide. I would remind the reader that memory of past lives, which is normally lost on incarnation, is regained by everyone on return to spirit.

Our past lives are shown on the timeline. Tay is the spirit guide in the current incarnation. The "missing" one of the Three in each life is the one who remained behind as the guide to the other two. As the reader may recall from the first book, two of the three incarnate and the one remaining behind is the guide. There is not a strict rotation about this; the Three decide between themselves who will go and who will stay.

As a point of explanation, the time spent back in spirit can vary from just a few years to several centuries of our Earth years. Time is not experienced in spirit in the same way as we experience it as humans. Our guide advised that eight months and eighty years are hardly different to spirit. Going on from this, a large time gap can be seen between some of our incarnations. In the first book I related that not all incarnations are on Earth, normally only a small proportion are, and most are spent elsewhere. I have included only one of these "elsewhere" lives in the timeline. Accepting reincarnation is a huge conceptual leap, an even larger one is to accept life elsewhere, so I do not elaborate on those alien lives beyond the one example.

COMMON CHARACTERISTICS

Lives taken on Earth do have some common features; some of these can be observed in my own past lives as follows:

- ❖ The roles of the two incarnating spirit one-thirds can be quite varied. They can be husband and wife, but may just as likely be, as my own lives show in other roles, master and student, family member, even prostitute and client!
- ❖ Use is made of a complete range of experiences in the human condition, from a wealthy ship owner to a street urchin, from life in a primitive tribal society to that of the modern west.
- ❖ Incarnations can be in any culture. I have for example, been English, Irish, French, Japanese and Middle Eastern. Spiritually we are indeed all one. A few brave individuals

have spoken out about the equality of man, regardless of colour, race or creed, but the majority sadly, do not see themselves as equal.
- ❖ Violent death is not a rare occurrence. War, earthquake, drowning and execution have at least once been my means of shuffling off the mortal coil.
- ❖ Whilst the phrase "soul groups" can be misleading, it is quite common to meet those with whom one has shared one or more past lives. This phenomenon explains the feeling of familiarity one sometimes has with a person without quite understanding why.

EVOLUTION OF MAN

My earliest past life, though not particularly interesting from a spiritual perspective, is very much so in the context of human evolution and the debate about when modern man first walked on Earth. I never felt comfortable with the scientific explanation of life evolving spontaneously, even less so with the Christian concept of six days being all the time taken to create life. Our guide confirmed that, as I already believed, life was introduced onto planet Earth and did not spontaneously evolve or arise in accordance with Christian creationist belief. The very first life forms were introduced and allowed to evolve and then later, when it was observed that the evolution was not taking the path expected, Homo sapiens was introduced.

I was curious when spirit first incarnated here. There are those who believe recognisable human beings first evolved five hundred thousand to three million years ago. Yes they did, but they were not human as we are today. Spirit of the level that incarnates as human, first incarnated on Earth approximately 9000BC. Prior to that time, any life form was of the spiritual level that would now incarnate as animal, advised our guide. That perhaps explains why modern man, in the sense of the level of culture and technology, only occupies such a short space of time compared to a very long pre-history.

At what point did recognisable humans arrive on the planet? The second time life was introduced was around 7500BC. The life form we refer to as Neanderthal, was the evolutionary end of the first life introduced. It evolved directly from Homo erectus who in turn evolved the ape family. Our guide continued, *"If I interpret your chain of thought correctly, modern man Homo sapiens sapiens, did not evolve from the Neanderthal man, but was introduced as a 'new variety'. There was an overlapping period following the introduction of modern man during which Neanderthals gradually disappeared"*.

There is a scientific hypothesis that it was the advantage modern humans had in being nimble fingered that drove technological advances and behaviour that led to modern humans pushing Neanderthals to extinction. I wondered if there is any truth in this hypothesis.

Our guide replied that the hypothesis is not strictly correct. Once the "new variety" had established and was obviously evolving far faster than the old, spirit found it more useful to incarnate into this life form. As the only reason for any life form is as a vessel for a soul, once souls no longer require that style of vessel, it will become extinct. There were some experiences still to be had incarnating into a dying species, but once Homo sapiens sapiens was established, it was time for life on the planet to move on again. Indirectly, the fact that the new species was more agile and had a quicker brain pattern did result in the extinction of the old species, but because spirit no longer wanted the "old model", not for the reasons the scientists will put forward, he concluded.

I now set out details of our earthly spiritual biography.

NEOLITHIC 7994-7962BC: Our guide related that the life we refer to as Neolithic, was the first incarnation on Earth for our Three and was shared by our guide Tay and myself.

We were brothers (that is in the limited meaning that we were the offspring of the same mother). The area in which we lived was an oasis that has since been known as Jericho. We particularly chose to incarnate into such a backward environment so that on return to spirit we could experience this as a contrast to the evolved worlds into which we had hitherto been used to incarnating.

This was a time when feelings for another were very raw and unrefined, but despite this, the brothers had a closeness. This of course was the result of their spiritual connection. Our guide was the older brother and defended me, his younger sibling, who was weak of stature and did not survive as long as he did.

Due to the limited experiences of the life, there were not great leaps to be made spiritually in the incarnated form, but the lessons from it were always planned to have meaning on return to the spirit state. The life offered an example of the overriding attachment of two spiritual thirds. In this experience a spiritual connection was felt to some degree by the brothers, even though the vessels containing their spirits for the life were not evolved enough to even form the thought, let alone understand it.

PAKISTAN 2302-2254BC: Angie was Amhika, a worker of cotton cloth in what our archaeologists now call Mohenjo Daro, an important city situated near the River Indus in what we know as Pakistan. Our guide was Tshoka, her husband in that life. He lived 2310-2244BC and worked in the city granary as a labourer.

They both died of natural causes in this incarnation. They had a shared sadness, as Amhika could not carry a child to term. All her brother's wives and her own sister managed this without difficulty as did our guide's own brothers wives and sisters. This inability was a shame in that culture. She was seen as a lesser woman and our guide was encouraged to take another partner. In their culture at the time, the reason for paring was only procreation of the race, emotion rarely entered into it. Tshoka loved Amhika, however, and would not consider the proposal and so shared her shame in the eyes of their families.

The lessons of this life were that one should not allow the expectations of others to influence one's behaviour. If you have ideals, do not be afraid to "wear your heart on your sleeve" and suffer the derision of others in following your own path. You and only you are the shaper of your destiny. The only other who should have an input in this is your other third. Even then, it is possible for one incarnated third to complete their plan while the other does not, so the ultimate responsibility for your destiny rests in your own hands. *"You should not be swayed from your ideals by the opinions of those who know not the content of your head and heart"*, concluded our guide.

We have had an enquirer for mediumship with almost exactly this same life-plan. Her family coincidentally, is of Pakistan origin, but she is westernised, having been born in the UK and attended a local state school with only a small Asian contingent. She is now in her thirties, and has come under intense family pressure to consent to an arranged marriage, it being considered a disgrace to her family to have a child of that age unmarried.

She is sufficiently spiritually aware to know she has what she terms a "soul-mate", but is not aware who this is, or indeed, if they have even met yet. She is consequently most distressed at being subjected to family pressure. During mediumship it was confirmed that she had planned that she would discover her Third late in her life and would experience the family and cultural pressure to marry as a spiritual test.

My personal comment on Angie's past life as Amhika is that the "stage prop" of infertility is still current, over four thousand years later. There can still be peer pressure to have children experienced by young women, as well as family pressure sometimes. Close to home, my brother and his wife were biologically unable to have children, a source of much disappointment. This was, of course, part of their life-plan, although not exactly the same lesson as in this past life, but the "tool" was the same.

EGYPT 1704-1671BC: Angie was Kia, handmaiden in the temple of Isis, who the Egyptians worshipped as the mother goddess, Queen of the underworld, and who they believed to be especially protective of women and children. Kia took the temple name of Ankhesenisis, which means, "She lives in Isis". She lived approximately 1706-1682BC. Our guide was her brother Tjelamunra and lived approximately 1704-1671BC. He was a priest in training in the temple of Ra. In this life, they both gave themselves to a life of devotion, or at least, that was the intention.

Before going further, our guide digressed and commented generally on ancient Egypt. He advised that our archaeologists research much into the life of these times, but they do so only with their limited scientific knowledge. The need to see, feel and touch in order to believe and their resistance to accept what at times, stares them right in the face is an impediment to their discovery of what the truth really is.

Our guide went on to say that in order to fully understand the life of the times it is necessary to understand that the ruling class, the wise men and the priests, who were really teachers rather than priests in the first instance, were originally not of the planet. They were visitors. True, they reproduced on our planet for a number of years, and in doing so, absorbed human characteristics into their culture and make-up. They also had new arrivals from the home world throughout the time of the visit.

   When they realised that they were not visiting at the right time, that Earth was not ready for their enlightenment and that with the interbreeding, their race was being taken backwards, rather than the people of Earth advanced, they departed in what relatively speaking, was quite a short space of time.

   The race was highly evolved and spiritually enlightened in many ways. In my first book I identified Jesus as a spiritual master, and as we know of course, the world in which we live has turned him and his teachings into a religion. Our guide explained that much the same happened in the Egyptian culture, that those we now interpret as gods worshipped by the Egyptians, were in fact originally the spiritual masters that the people had identified during their history. According to our guide, these people identified the masters among them in their home world and revered their teachings and celebrated their wisdom. On Earth, however, the human element crept in again and turned them into gods, attributing to them myth and legend. This was a contributing factor in the ruling class decision to leave Earth.

   In chapter six I discuss an enquirer's life in ancient Egypt, one that predates this particular Egyptian life of our Three. In the life under discussion, the main lessons that the incarnation was designed to teach were: the denial of self in the pursuit of pure spirituality, the moving into the spiritual while in the physical; the leaving of a material existence to work for spirit.

   Our guide related that he had guided his sister (Angie) into her role in the temple of Isis. She suffered death from a snakebite and was returned to spirit before completing her desired level of communication and of denial of self. (This possibly explains her revulsion for the creatures in this current life.)

   It was responsible for her failing to complete her task and forced a repeat. Of course, the accident shortening her life was in her plan. Where she had failed was in the degree of progression she had attained by the time it occurred. She started slowly, choosing the pleasures of the physical life in preference to the spiritual path that awaited her and perhaps would not have started at all if it had not been for the guidance of our guide, then her younger sibling. This is an excellent example of freewill choice upsetting a life-plan to the point of a repeat incarnation being required.

In *"Why Come Back?"* I wrote that in some races on other planets, what we term as suicide is in fact the accepted normality. Once the tasks of the incarnation are complete, once you are not required to provide interaction with your third or any other incarnated being anymore, it would be considered incorrect to remain in the incarnation. The reasoning is that one should hasten back to the spiritual state to speed the incarnation into the next life, the quicker to promote the eventual return to the Collective. In such a life, failing to end one's life at the required time would be seen as a failure. This is not the way we interpret things! As I have said so often, a change of perspective alters everything.

Our guide did not explain the following to us at the time of giving us this information, as we had not at that time received the necessary teaching to understand it. He has since added the following however, to complete the picture of that life. He related that such a situation was the case on the home planet and was the case initially in the time we refer to as Ancient Egypt. It was something else that lost its way following time and interbreeding. It accounts for what our scholars now mistakenly see as the Egyptian preoccupation with death.

Tjelamunra related that he achieved his objectives early in the incarnation, and having completed his task should have returned to spirit. He had developed an illicit loving relationship with a young girl and did not wish to leave her. This was a real slip up. True, it was a pre-planned freewill choice, but one he failed to negotiate in the desired manner.

He further related that this was an example of a failure at the first attempt by both incarnated thirds. The life was not a success for either Angie or himself. She failed to start her spiritual work soon enough in life to complete the planned level before suffering the snakebite that ended her life. She learned on return to spirit, some degree of the nature of love from his care for her spiritual enlightenment, but really, the incarnation was not successful.

Tjelamunra, the then incarnated spirit, now our guide, completed his required level of enlightenment, but lost what he had gained by developing the attachment. This was a freewill choice, which was planned as a further lesson in the true nature of love. He allowed that to take precedence over his planned return to spirit. He was tormented by guilt over this and eventually took the correct course of action, but several years after it was correct for him to do so. Although he learned something of love and attained a level of enlightenment, he failed in the freewill choice to identify his correct path. *"No,"* he corrected, *"worse than that, I identified it but ignored it and took the pleasures of the physical instead"*. Both lives were an example of a freewill choice taken that occasioned a repeat incarnation.

CRETE 1524-1470BC: Our guide related that I was Philon, a sailor living in what is now Crete and which was at that time part of the Minoan civilisation. This was during the time it enjoyed its greatest prosperity due to its mastery of the sea. Angie was Tyche, 1528-1484BC, a lady of the night for whom I formed an attachment and a feeling of protectiveness.

I had no thoughts of making the relationship permanent; sailors did not do so at that time, until ready to leave the sea. I did however visit her on every available occasion. I feared for her safety and tried to encourage her to leave the life she led. My fears were well grounded as, during one of my voyages, she was stabbed by a patron and died. Although her life-style was a disreputable one, the goodness of her soul shone through and this was the attraction for me.

The lessons of this life were that a person of spiritual enlightenment does not have to lead a life of pure chastity in order to gain spiritual progression on return to spirit; that one should look beyond the outward physical, and search for the inner spiritual. Our guide confirmed that both of us learned this lesson well in this life, which was a hard life for the both of us. We did not view it as such at the time, however, having no expectation of anything better.

NEAR-EAST 1046-1004BC: I was Abisha, a scribe for a merchant in the Hebrew city of Har Megiddo on the Nahal Iron Pass. Our guide was my brother Abijah, a potter. This was the only route where chariots could speed between Egypt and Syria. A major earthquake struck along a fault system in the earth in 1004BC and the city was destroyed in the earthquake. Abisha and Abijah both perished in the disaster.

Our guide related that in this life, I was initially envious of my master the merchant. I saw his lifestyle and his riches, which contrasted greatly with the simple life led by my brother and myself. Neither of us married, but lived in the family home right until the time of the disaster. I did, however, come to understand that no amount of physical riches can purchase peace for the soul.

My master's wife, Adina, was younger than her husband and much given to disporting herself with the charioteers that passed through the city. The master, although aware of her infidelity, suffered it in silence, rather than risk losing her altogether, but his pain was immense. I saw this and was appreciative of the lesson I learned in the incarnation. Both the master and his wife perished in the quake and, of course, the lesson on return to spirit, was that the riches of the soul amassed whilst in the physical serve one well on return to spirit, whereas the riches of the physical are just that and nothing else.

SUDAN 920-873BC: Our guide explained that in this life I was Bahska, a Nubian living in Napata in Kush. Angie was my wife Raka. This was a fairly uneventful life; we met, joined our lives and had two sons.

It may be of interest to note that one of these is my son in the current life. The lessons learned were those of love and support of each other and of providing for our sons. One of them experienced early death due to illness and this was a tragedy we shared, from which we learned closeness and support of each other.

It is of personal interest to note that the younger son has been my earthly brother in this life. He seems to prefer the role of being the cause of grief! (This life has two examples of the "familiar actor" phenomenon, which I discuss in chapter three.)

The other son went on to work in the household of the ruler Shabaka and this was a source of pride for us both. For Angie, this explained the closeness she feels to my son, who is not her own in this life. For me, it explained the feeling that my son is more spiritual than my other children. He is an older spirit, true, but the real feeling is the familiarity of spirit that I feel with him.

Our lives both ended by natural causes. Our guide concluded by saying that this was one of the many "average" lives necessary to make up the full picture, but we noted that even in that life, a little rain fell.

GREECE 810-744BC: I was Eudamidas, a Phoenician ship owner. I grew wealthy through trade and my lifestyle was quite luxurious. I wanted for nothing and was not used to having my wishes thwarted in any way. I did not use my wealth for the benefit of others and showed impatience with the less fortunate, or those of little intelligence, and those I considered to be beneath my concern. It was of course, in my plan to allow this to occur so that the lesson of the incarnation would be fully learned by its contrast to the norm of my life.

This lesson was presented to me in the guise of the terminal illness of my only daughter and favourite child. She was a beautiful girl, accomplished and intelligent. I had allowed her an education usually only given to male children and delighted in her quick wit and her ability to converse with me on matters of business and political importance. When she became ill, I tried everything to prevent her decline. Through this I was made to realise that my money, my position and power were all trappings of the physical. The very thing I wanted most, to reverse the declining health of this much loved child, I was unable to achieve.

This was a great chance to learn, to acknowledge a poignant lesson in the physical. Unfortunately, I, Eudamidas, acted inappropriately and missed this great opportunity. My love of this child turned to resentment. I blamed her for causing me pain and anguish. I had the opportunity to support her with my love in her time of trial, to become closer to her as she prepared for return to spirit and to share this preparation. Instead of this I ignored her, refusing even to be in her company although she craved it. I could not accept that she, whom I loved, was the instrument that had "burst my bubble" and forced me to the realisation of my own mortality and the illusory value of my wealth and power.

Following her death, rather than cherish and preserve her memory, I had all trace of her obliterated from my home and my life. Her name was not allowed to be spoken within my hearing and on her day of birth each year, I would shut myself away. None of my family or servants dare approach me at this time. (This reaction of obliterating evidence of the deceased is reminiscent of the reaction of Angie's father and my father following the death of our respective mothers. A life lesson witnessed from the opposite side of the coin in this current life.)

Spiritual realisation came to me as Eudamidas on my own deathbed. I realised the waste of the incarnation, realised the lessons I had been presented with and repented my actions. Although I had missed, to some degree, a learning opportunity, I did in fact realise the lesson while still in the physical, just! It did require a repeat, however, as the lesson was not completed satisfactorily.

Our guide was the daughter of this incarnation, living from 782 to 766BC, a mere sixteen years. Her lessons were the suffering of terminal illness and of coming to a state of peace about her forthcoming departure from the physical. She suffered the pain of her beloved father withdrawing his love and affection from her when she needed it most. She should have seen the reasons, she had sufficient enlightenment to realise this was a manifestation of his grief and despair but instead she failed completely to understand his actions. She developed resentment in her turn and died with the hurt still in her heart, unable even on the point of death to grasp the lesson. Of course on return to spirit it was crystal clear, but she required a repeat too.

ITALY 638-589BC: I was Acreisus, an Etruscan who lived in Cortina. I was a student in the art of casting and fashioning statues for the nobility, the materials I specialised in being bronze and clay.

Our guide related the life as follows: *Acreisus thought himself fortunate to be studying under a renowned Greek named Sopatros, a master craftsman, but there was a price to the honour of being this man's student. Although gifted in his art, the master was no student of human nature and taught by tyranny and authoritarianism. Any student who was misfortunate enough to come within his control feared him. A gifted, talented man, but without spirituality. He always had two students at any given time and the other student sharing the tuition with Acreisus was Gaios, in fact the spirit incarnated in this current life as your mother.*

Acreisus became a master of his art by the age of thirty and had students under tuition himself. In contrast to the treatment he had received from Sopatros, he taught with compassion and respect, which earned him the esteem and admiration of his own students.

I (our guide) *was a student under Acreisus named Theotimos and lived* **624-560BC.** *I showed a particular genius and Acreisus was drawn to me with a particular fondness. It would be true to say that he loved me as the son he was never likely to have, as he had chosen a single life in pursuit of his art.*

The major plot of this incarnation was the lesson learned from the contrast in the styles of the two teachers, Sopatros and Acreisus. Both had considerable skill and both had the desire to teach and pass on this skill to others. The difference was that Sopatros was frightened and jealous that he may be usurped by one of his own students, and thought that by seeking to control and break their spirit he could subjugate them so that they would not seek to surpass him.

Acreisus, however, showed his spirituality in his teaching. He shared of his knowledge unstintingly, rejoicing in the skill of those he taught. He opened his heart to his students, shared in their triumphs and failures, carefully nurtured their blossoming talent till it came into full bloom and could stand alone. He took pride and pleasure in the talent of those he taught, rather than fearing it.

The lesson for me (our guide) *was in observing the free spirit within my master, to observe the munificence with which the teacher gave of his very self in his teaching. He gave away to his students the bounty of his talent and wisdom without seeking to gain any personal glory through their achievements.*

I gained from the bond with my master, was closer to him than I had been to my own father, and learned to some degree the difference between a biological and spiritual connection.

ET LIFE: This is the only one example we have been allowed to have, of an extraterrestrial life, which I now describe. The incarnation was *approximately* 2050 of our years ago. Our guide, in order to explain it to us, needed to relate it to an earthly life so that we may understand it. He hoped we would be able to grasp that the life itself was completely unlike anything we have here on Earth and that things such as the "job description" were given only as a means of explaining the concepts of this life to us.

I was an historian who wrote detailed papers, which were treated with respect. I worked in the equivalent of a university and taught student historians. My specialist subject, on which I was considered something of an expert apparently, was the last war the planet had experienced. That was some thousands of years before my incarnation, as the planet had a great degree of spirituality and had not experienced war for a long time even then.

Communication with spirit was a natural event in that world and was the source of the information for my work. I would otherwise not have had such accurate and detailed information to impart. Our guide gave us a comparison in that much as in this current life, someone whose subject is the Second World War will be able to give much more accurate and confirmed information than one whose subject is the Battle of Hastings. The latter will be less detailed due to the passing of time. If, however, the scholar detailing the Battle of Hastings could have spiritual communication to tell him how it was, if his students and peers accepted this communication unquestionably, then how much more complete his knowledge and therefore his work would be. This was the way of it for me then.

Our guide continued by advising that all persons incarnating on that planet had the ability for spiritual communication. It was just so much a part of their everyday life. The scholars and academics had the ability to a greater degree; the degree of this ability was what was used as a measure of their "intelligence" for want of a better description, much as the awarding of my degree signifies my intelligence in this incarnation.

Our guide could not give me my name from that time, as our language does not support it. He could, however, tell me that my sister in that life was our spiritual sister, my partner Angie. Families on that planet stayed together for the length of their incarnation, the offspring of the female members joined the existing family. There was no life pairing such as we have.

The only time a "new" family was created was when there were no more female members to add to an existing one. At that point remaining male members would apply for permission to start a new line, with a female member from another household which had become rich with female members and who was prepared to leave her own family branch to become a much revered family founder. Quite a different way of life and continuance of species to that on Earth.

The people were a gentle, loving, spiritual race, highly evolved and intelligent. Due to this family formation, brothers and sisters were close to each other and supportive of each other, much as life partners are on Earth. Our guide went on to relate that to be an academic among these people was to have reached the pinnacle of achievement. The majority of spirit incarnating there is level three and above, although a scattering of lower levels may incarnate there for specific reasons.

I lived a long life of sixty of our Earth years, the average lifespan on the planet being fifty-four of our years. I sired ten offspring, but did not know them, as was the custom. I did not feel bereft by this, as it was the accepted way. The children I would have felt bereft if separated from, would be the children of the female members of my family group, my sister's children for instance. I had four other sisters, but was spiritually close to my spiritual sister, as I knew her to be my spirit third. Her son followed me as an historian, making him dear to me.

Our guide said that this was perhaps not a biography that I expected, but it explained some of my interests and indicates how spiritual awareness is advanced in other worlds. In my current life, history was my favourite subject at school. I almost went on to take it as a degree. Historical documentaries are favourite TV viewing. Whilst I could "rationalise" my interest in history as the subject which helps best explain the present world, I never dreamt of an extraterrestrial past life explanation. Like other aspects of ourselves that create so much of our characters, occupation and hobbies can have a hidden depth of explanation in past lives.

An aside here would be to reconsider the popular notion that aliens wish us harm, or have a control agenda. Some of the most popular films of modern times have this theme, *"Star Wars"*, *"Independence Day"* and many more. What is not generally appreciated is, that our assumption alien life would follow the human pattern in our aggression and warlike behaviour is falsely based. Wars are only found on the nursery worlds. Higher evolved worlds have worked through the base instinct phase and go on to enjoy a more spiritually based culture. We have our evidence for this on Earth. Some of the older tribes of North America, before the white man's diseases extinguished them, had long forsaken war.

BRAZIL AD1247-90: We were told of the life led by Angie and I in Brazil as follows: I was Fet who lived 1247-90 and Angie was Jeh, 1249-73. We were bonded as partners in 1262 and had five children.

The tribe was called Ipicas. The life was simple, the village consisting of a ring of mud huts with a type of thatch roof. They grew a little food but hunted for most. The village had its chief and a council. Although the chief's word was the law in all day-to-day decisions and running of affairs, the council had to be approached to give opinions or decisions of any great moment. As so often is the case, the older members of council were set in their ways and resisted all change, just because it was change, and for the sake of resisting, rather than for any logical reason. These elders always resisted my father, the chief, and the younger council members, who recognised the need to advance the culture.

I was the second son of the family, the first born being the heir to the chief of the village, but being completely incapable of the task due to mental instability. Our father, the chief, wished to break with tradition for the good of the tribe and make me, Fet, his heir. Some on the council did not agree, mainly the older members who were steeped in tradition and would object to anything, no matter how logical, that defied tradition.

From this life, I learned sympathy with mental illness; I developed a need to understand it, an inbuilt desire to know its causes and effects. As Fet, my guide told me, I had loved my brother dearly. Although the younger, I had been the protector of my older sibling, due to his mental incapacity. I had to accept the fact that I was to replace my brother due to the mental illness, something I found difficult because of my love for him. I had to learn that what I initially thought of as an act of unfaithfulness towards my brother was in fact an act of kindness and compassion. The lesson being, of course, that by replacing him as chief, I was in fact protecting him from the life it was impossible for him to live.

Our guide explained that Jeh died young, leaving behind her five motherless children for Fet to raise. She knew for some time that she was dying and learned much of the nature of mother love from this. She learned from being denied the opportunity to practice it, as much as from the practising of it. She learned the lesson of leaving children, knowing she was not going to be able to care for them and that they would grow up without her. She suffered from this and more fully learned the nature of mother love. She also held her husband in high regard and felt pain at the thought of adding to his burden, which was already great. She supported him and agonised with him over the replacing of his brother. He was subject to the demands of being chief, a role he did not assume easily due to his feelings about his brother, and then had to deal with her loss and the care of five children. It would have been customary to take a second wife, but he did not, as such was his regard for her, he preferred to remain without a partner.

The lesson from this aspect of the life was learned on return to spirit. Jeh was shown that he could have taken a partner to help him with the care of the children, and to give him comfort and support and that this would not have been a betrayal of the love and regard for his wife, would not have been an offence to her memory. As they were two incarnated one thirds, no one else would have offered him what they shared physically and spiritually but someone else could have comforted him in his incarnation and this would not have been wrong. The lesson about the nature of love is that one can feel different love for different people within one's life, and that feeling love for one does not necessarily prohibit feelings for another or lessen their value.

By way of endnotes, this life is one of the two lives that I had images of when I had my past life regression experience. This was because it was an important incarnation for me. I saw myself in a primitive tribal setting, mud floors, forest surrounding the village. I saw children running barefoot, saw my wife, her face indistinct. A village election was taking place, or so it seemed, and I felt a great excitement. I now know my interest in mental health in my current life and my fascination with birds originated here, in this past life. Two aspects of my make-up are thus explained. Interesting too, is the fact our friends have a four year old son, to whom I instantly took a liking. This is unusual in itself, as I usually have more rapport with older children. Upon enquiry of our guide, I am advised he was my brother in this Brazilian life.

CHAPTER TWO

FURTHER CASE STUDY PAST LIVES

In order to complete my own spiritual biography of lives spent on Earth, I now continue with the remaining ones. At the end of the chapter is my "timeline" summary of all lives. This could be constructed for any of our enquirers for mediumship, except to say it is quite time-consuming to do so. What I have experienced is nothing unique. I repeat, I use my own lives as a case study to show how we all have complex make-ups to our inner being; we are all pilgrims on the journey of spiritual experience.

The Bard, as usual, was able to put spiritual concepts into poetry. In addition to the famous line in *"As You Like It"* of *"All the world's a stage"*, he went on to say, *"And one man in his time plays many parts"*. When I was a young man searching to know myself and better understand the world, I had no thought of reincarnation as an explanatory tool. It is so very difficult in the modern West to find and accept this fundamental truth. As my guide might say, the added challenge is afforded by this culture!

FRANCE 1318-40: Our guide gave us the following summary: I was Ansel, born in Poitiers in France in 1318. I went to work as a mariner and volunteered to fight in the Battle of Sluys in the summer of 1340, during which I lost my life. My father had predeceased me but I left my mother and one sister alive in Poitiers.

In that battle, I fought with the French under Barbnoir and Quiriel. I was on the great cog Christopher; cog was the term for the boat at the time. This boat had been captured from the English by the French but was retaken by the English during this battle. At the time of its capture it was full of French, Geonese, Piccards and Castilians. The outcome of the battle was decided in just two hours but raged on for a total of eight. The English had archers, crossbow men, and men-at-arms that fought hand-to-hand using grapples, hooks and iron chains.

When the outcome of the battle was obvious, and on the taking of the Christopher by the English, I, together with some others, swam ashore. On landing, the Flemish, who were on the side of the English, clubbed us to death. It was a long time before news of my demise reached my remaining family, although my mother, to whom I was particularly close, had "sensed" my death at the time of it occurring, almost to the hour. She suddenly felt the loss of this son to whom she had a remarkable closeness. It is then not surprising that the mother was my current partner Angela and my other third. She was Alba and lived from 1299 to 1358 and was an important influence on my life.

During this life the lessons taught were the loss of a parent, which caused great suffering to my mother, the person I cared for most in the world. I learned that pain in a loved one can be harder to bear than pain in oneself. I learned the type of love demonstrated by loyalty to a cause, and again, at the point of death was conscious of the pain I in my turn would be causing to my mother, pain that I would have spared her if I could at all.

The lesson for our sister was the lesson of mother love, loss as a mother of her precious child to a senseless war that was not even really his to fight! She loved and lost her husband, and experienced that too. The main lesson however, was her attachment to me, and my subsequent loss.

INDIA 1480-96: I had a short life in India at the time of the Mogul Empire, as Namdev. In this life I was left orphaned together with my two brothers Harshul and Eknath, when illness took both parents, my much loved sister Behula and other brother Asad. Our guide related that together with my brothers I lived on the streets, surviving only by our wits and what we could steal. This unfortunately was my undoing as I was caught stealing food and executed for this.

From this life I learned the benefit of the support of parents and the protection of a family unit by being without this. Our guide has previously said in an explanation of the need to experience both sides of a coin to understand a given lesson, that one needs to know what it is to have food and what it is not to have food in order to fully understand hunger. One half of the lesson was certainly put to good use here!

I was subjected to the trauma of loosing loved ones, particularly my sister to whom I was very close. I experienced responsibility through love by having to assume responsibility for my brothers at a very young age. The opportunity was given to me to abandon them and look after myself only, but I made the correct freewill choice and followed the path of caring for them to the best of my ability.

I had a sharp intelligence, our guide said; a trait shared with my sister of the life, and I was frustrated by my inability to use it given my social standing, or rather lack of it. I saw about me those with little intelligence, little appreciation of anything other than their own comfort, having the resources to enjoy the books and art treasures that I would have appreciated so much given the chance, and learned that having money does not necessarily bequeath the intelligence to enjoy for the right reasons that which money can bring.

A short, sharply painful life, but one in which I acquitted myself well according to our guide. Stealing in order to survive does not jeopardise spiritual progression!

ENGLAND 1537-1603: Our guide summarised this life as follows: *"Roger and Angie were Thomas and Anne Roper, who were married in April 1559. She was born in 1539 and died in 1597 and he was born in 1537 and died in 1603. They had four children, Thomas born March 1560, Anne born June 1561, Catherine born February 1564 and Henry born September 1569.*

They had been lovers from the time of Anne attaining the age of fourteen, but her father was sickly and her mother had died at her birth. Anne, being the only child and a girl, was required to remain at home to nurse her father who had never remarried due to his health and his continuing grief over his wife who he had genuinely loved. From this she learned the nature of two different kinds of love, the love and respect she held for her father, the devotion that meant she kept to her duty of care for him, and the love she felt for Thomas, which was akin to the sharing of her very soul with him.

Thomas was a scribe employed in the keeping of ledgers for a cloth merchant. He had an income, not large, but dependable. On the death of her father, Anne inherited his estate, however, and this enabled the couple to start life together in the year of Elizabeth I's coronation, 1559. Thomas learned that love should be open and giving. That one should look to the happiness of the object of the love as the truest way of expressing it, and not follow one's own selfish desires in the mistaken belief that it shows one's love of the other.

By allowing Anne to remain with her father during his incapacity, by waiting a time for her to be free for marriage, he acted unselfishly. He put his own wishes into the background and supported his love in her devotion, knowing that he had a strong enough hold on her affections to demand that she acted against her conscience, but realising that he would sour her love if he demanded that she do so.

They were both spiritually aware in this life. However, their young life was spent through a period of religious turmoil, with the religion of the country swinging first from the Protestant Edward to the Catholic Mary and then back to the Protestant Elizabeth. Being of a spiritual awareness meant that they could easily, and without trouble to their conscience, follow the dictates of the time as required. They knew the real truth and were therefore able to assume the role required to ensure their survival and that of their family. The lesson from this was of course that it matters not what men say with their lips, it is what they know and believe in their head and heart, in their spirit, that really matters. That survival of the body is not incorrect as long as it is not at the expense of others.

They knew that they were not alone in their enlightenment, that there were others, William Shakespeare for one, whom they believed shared their spirituality and beliefs. They looked for the subliminal messages of these others to strengthen their own beliefs, much as the two of you now read the writings of others and rejoice when you find confirmation of your own truths within the pages. Roger has been accurate in his identification of these messages, but of course, he has identified them once before" our guide teased!

JAPAN 1628-95: Our life was summarised as follows: I was Enku, a Japanese artist-priest who took a vow to sculpt 120,000 images of the Buddha. Our guide shared this incarnation as a novice to the priest. His name was Dai. He assisted with the sculpting and we were constantly together during many years. The vow was not met, but I gave my whole life to the task, which was the intended plan. During this life my belief was that such a vow would direct my attention and my thoughts totally to matters spiritual, to the teaching of my master, Buddha, and that in so doing my spiritual advancement would be hastened.

This of course was not the case. Pursuit of the fulfilment of the vow became my obsession. I thought not so much on the teachings of my Buddha, but more on how to complete the next sculpture, and the next, and the next. I lost sight of the reason for the vow in my endeavours to complete it.

On return to spirit, I saw that spiritual enlightenment and advancement is not to be gained by following another's way, but by finding the way for oneself. Further, that the pursuit of any goal that has as its reason only satisfaction or glorification of self, even if that goal purports to have spiritual reasoning behind it, is not the way to achieve growth of spirit.

Our guide drew a comparison with our current lives. He asked us to think on our endeavours in this life; yes we will both achieve satisfaction of self in our spiritual work, but the purpose will be seen to us both as the bringing of the information to others; as the learning for self while helping others to learn; the receipt of enlightened growth, of freedom for the soul, while helping others to reach this state of peace within themselves. *"Love of your fellow man and the just desire to assist in the enlightenment of others, even if those others are a comparatively small number in the global scheme, will result in you achieving what we earnestly strive to give out"* our guide indicated. *"You will be aware this time,"* he said, *"that the pursuit of the task should not become the obsession, to the exclusion of the reason for the undertaking in the first place."*

Finally, our guide related that he learned from watching his master, Enku, in his obsessive pursuit, and by being driven to help him at all costs without understanding why he did so. He learned the lesson, not by experiencing it himself, but by his close contact with the one that did. This as we know is often the case. Of course, on return to spirit I was immediately aware of the lesson I could not see on Earth, and learned greatly from the experience.

Why Come Back? Book 2

ENGLAND 1735-81: Our guide gave these details: I was Tobias Furneaux, born Aug 1735 and died September 1781. I was born at Swilley, near Portsmouth, but lived in Cornwall for most of my life.

As Tobias, I sailed on many noteworthy journeys and was noted as the first explorer to circumnavigate the world in both directions. I sailed on a westerly-directed circumnavigation in the ship "HMS Dolphin" in 1766 and was one of the first Europeans to reach Tahiti. I was the Captain of the ship "HMS Adventure" on Cook's second voyage to the Pacific in 1771. I explored and charted the south coast of Tasmania. In New Zealand, ten of my crew were captured and killed by Maoris. As Maoris were cannibals at that time it was apparently my belief that they would have been eaten, and this was something that troubled me greatly. My other major command was of the "HMS Syren" in the British attack on Charleston, in 1776, during the American War of Independence.

Our guide was my servant, named after me and my place of birth, Tobias Swilley. He was, according to our guide, with me for many years, and up to the time of my death. He nursed me through my trouble with gout on more than one occasion. Our guide reflected he was shown greater kindness and esteem than it was common to expect for one in his position. His master talked to him as a friend rather than a servant, and he would have visited the very gates of hell for Furneaux (me) had he asked it of him.

I apologise to the reader for a touch of vanity here. I would like to quote one of James Cook's biographers, Richard Hough, who gave this thumbnail portrait: *"He (Furneaux) showed himself as highly responsible and although there was one serious fracas with the Tahitians, he later cemented friendship with the natives by tact and restraint. His personality did not match the power and colour of Cook's and he was a touch weak on discipline, but he was a good man to sail with and much liked by those who did".*

Our guide related that the lessons of that life were many. One of the greatest for me as Tobias was the pain and anguish I suffered over the loss of ten crew in New Zealand. I held myself responsible and the fact that I believed them eaten, troubled me more than perhaps death of any other kind might have done. I learned on return to spirit, that one chooses one's own path, that one human cannot be held accountable for the experiences of another.

I was considered a touch lax on discipline but that was a product, our guide said, of my kindness and respect for my crew, which was above the norm for the time. True, my failure to force the more ignorant among them to adhere to the correct diet led to scurvy on board, a fact I was berated for by others, but my nature did not easily accept the forcing of my will onto others. This was due to my spirituality. I believed at that stage in freewill choice, had an understanding of this, and therefore found it difficult to administer what others thought of as discipline for the good of those under their command.

I learned on return to spirit to see the two sides of the coin. On the one hand, much falsehood, much cruelty and barbarity have been committed under the guise of "what is good" for others. Take the reign of Mary Tudor in which hundreds were subject to cruel torture and burning in the name of "leading them back to the *true* religion", when in fact we know that no religion is true. On the other hand, teaching others to eat a diet to promote their health, a diet that due to choice of birth and education you know is correct, and by choice of birth and education, they do not, is not the same. If once sure that they understand the reasoning, that they are in possession of the facts, they still choose to ignore the information, then that of course is their freewill choice. Sometimes it is necessary to illustrate by example, however. This was my lesson too.

I later captained my ship in attack on others. This I found alien to my soul and I ended my career at sea because of my distaste for it. Our guide summarised, *"A kindly and gentle soul, out of place in the environment he had chosen for himself to live, but from his spiritual perspective, a life that provided much in the way of enlightenment and growth".*

Such is often the case when one finds oneself as a square peg in a round hole. Contrast is a great teacher. He continued by saying that other main lessons from this lifetime were, that one does not need to exert pressure over others, even when in a position of seniority. If those for whom one has responsibility are touched by kindness, they will respond through respect rather than fear. Also, his gentle handling of his other third, who was in a position not usually expecting of gentle handling, touched them both. He saw the slave trade at close quarters, but managed never to be involved in it. He reviled a practice that treated another soul in this manner, again a mark of his spirituality and another lesson learned.

The lessons I learned as Furneaux, our guide learned too, by sharing the experience, by being my confidant and so privy to the innermost thoughts, the battles with myself and my conscience. He learned from observation, by being in close contact with the one experiencing. This is often the case with thirds, one has the "colourful" life, the lion share of the tragedy etc, but the other lives in the shadow of it and learns by observation, or is drawn into it from a different perspective and so learns in that way. *"One of the major lives for the two of us,"* said our guide, *"No I am wrong to say that, all lives are just a step along the road, but some take a bigger stride than others, and the strides made by this one were worthy of a giant!"*

As endnotes (and further vanity) here, it is interesting that because I have been once someone of note, there is evidence of what I once looked like, as an oil portrait of Furneaux was commissioned. Some of those to whom I have shown a photograph of this portrait can see certain facial similarities. Similarly, a portrait exists of Francois Couperin, the harpsichord composer who I mentioned previously as being the seventeenth century previous incarnation of an enquirer. Although there is little similarity in his physical features, the character description of Couperin that accompanied the picture in a book of composers, is most certainly consistent with certain traits in his current life character!

It was fascinating for me to read an echo from my eighteenth century sea captain life in the British national press recently. It was reported on 30 November 2001, that a portrait by Sir Joshua Reynolds became the second most expensive British painting ever auctioned when it sold for £10.5 million at Sotheby's. The title was *"Portrait of Omai"*. As Captain Furneaux, I had brought Omai to England from Tahiti in 1774. Omai met King George III and was the talk of London society for a period, before he returned home.

IRELAND 1853-73: Our guide summarised this life by telling me that I was Sean O'Brislain and he was Liam O'Brislain (1842-73). We were brothers working on the British White Star steamship

"*Atlantic*". It sank off Nova Scotia killing 547 of which we were two.

We were brothers who had suffered much hardship in that life, the death of both parents, the death of our sister and younger brother. We had both worked on the ships from as soon as we were old enough to do so, to get away from our uncle who mistreated the pair of us. He, being the eldest got work on the boats first, by the good graces of a sailor who showed him kindness such as he had not come to expect. This sailor went some way towards dissipating our guide's distrust of the human race, which was strong in him by then because of the treatment he had received in his life up to that time. When he was settled in the work, he came to fetch me away to join him.

Our guide said that we learned much from that life, loss of loved ones, mistreatment at the hands of one who was a blood kin to us both, teaching that biological relationship does not necessarily mean love or even liking. He suffered the guilt as he died, of thinking himself responsible for my death. If he had not brought me to that boat, I would not have drowned. He realised on return to spirit that this was our destiny, and that he had nothing to reproach himself for, that he had acted out of love by doing this.

ENGLAND 1890-1917: Our guide related that I was Peter Crawford who was killed in Flanders at the Hindenberg line. He was George Taylor, born 1884 and died in 1916 during the battle of the Somme in August of that year.

George was a Sergeant and I, Peter, a Lance Corporal, but we became firm friends, as we were the only two Yorkshiremen in the regiment. George was shot during the fighting in August of 1916 and I, apparently at risk to my own life, got him to a field hospital although it was too late for George and he died from the wound to the stomach. I was later shot, but the wound would not necessarily have proved fatal if I had been found in time and received medical attention. The mud and prevailing conditions were so terrible that I was not discovered and laid where I fell until my life had drained away from me.

I had a younger sister called Sarah and two brothers Henry and James. My father Jack was killed at sea in 1915, which was the cause of great sadness to my mother Emily, who never really recovered from it. I had not enjoyed good relations with my father, who appeared to resent the close relationship I had with my mother. It is true in fact, confirmed our guide, that my father was jealous of me, his first born son, jealous of the attention I received as an infant from my mother, attention until that time that would have been his. This is often the case when a first child is born. The father has become accustomed to the change by the birth of subsequent children, but the initial resentment of the first-born keeps a barrier between them, sometimes for many years if not for their entire lives.

Our guide went on to say that this was an important life for us both, with many opportunities for spiritual advancement through the lessons presented. One important lesson was my relationship, or lack of it, with my father. It was a difficult relationship for the both of us. As I have explained Jack was jealous without realising why. This lead him to feel guilty about what he considered to be his "unnatural" feelings for his son, and in turn, because the feeling of guilt made him uncomfortable, he transferred the blame for that back to me, Peter.

This of course, was all at a subconscious level and only became clear to him on return to spirit. I, in my turn, spent my life in anger at my father and the lack of relationship I observed him have with his other children, and I then suffered guilt on my father's death because the relationship had not been better and guilt for the feelings I had about him. I felt deep down that the difficulty was not of my making, but still regretted the lack of a better relationship with my father.

I missed the spiritual growth from that life, of learning to forgive in younger spirits what is perceived as their lack of communication and understanding of you, to accept them and their faults and to realise that they are spiritual beginners with much to learn; to realise that you are part of that learning curve and that of course, you all planned it this way. On return to spirit I learned that a relationship with a parent can be purely biological, chosen in fact, for the lack of spiritual compatibility in order to demonstrate exactly that point. The lesson was learned in spirit but a repeat was needed on the earth plane.

First hand observation of war provided a major lesson for the incarnation too, its inhumanity and pointlessness. Observation at close quarters of the make-up of the human character, its weaknesses and strengths, made all the more vivid because of the inflated examples of traits of character and emotions presented by war: suffering, fear, elation, guilt, dread, responsibility, courage, resentment, cowardice, horror, panic, trepidation, torment, anguish, distress, euphoria, apprehension, excitement, desolation, bitterness, valour, pain, misery and so much more.

The life provided the lesson of a love that is not romantic or physical in any way, but more the meeting of what some term, your soul mate. Of recognising the attraction to another, in this case a comparative stranger, at a depth of your being that you do not understand. Of feeling such a regard for this other, that you would put at risk your own life in an attempt to preserve theirs. This feeling that you know this person, really know them, that you have spent years in their company even though you have only just met. In short, recognising your other third, and acknowledging that the attraction exists, exploring it in your mind.

Not realising the spiritual connection yet, that comes later in another life, but taking this first step. George and I, as Peter, attained this first step. George at his death actually realised the spiritual connection too, sufficiently to not require a second step in order to achieve that part. The further step is usually required to know the reason for the attraction, to understand that your connection is at a spiritual level and that this person is in fact part of you, and that you come from the same source.

Our guide went on to say that Peter and George did well in that life. True, I did not quite master the problem with my father, but that was only a sub-plot. I did make the necessary connection with George, and George with me, and so we completed the first step in that lesson successfully. George managed to complete the second stage to a sufficient degree and that is what Angela and I have achieved this time together.

The major plot for us, of course, was the learning from the war, all those many emotions and aspects that were presented to us, and we both achieved this well, being sufficiently sensitive spiritually, to appreciate these many facets.

SOME OBSERVATIONS

I am fond of reading obituaries in the broadsheet newspapers, to read in the case of ex-servicemen, what deeds of daring gave rise to their medals, or in the case of academics and business leaders, what their achievements were and how they came to make them. Of course, obituaries are not written in terms of spiritual growth and progression, which may have no connection with what is regarded as human achievement. Indeed, as my own lives indicate, those achieving greatest spiritual growth are most likely the unknowns, those whose achievements are private and personal, which appear transient, but are in fact, permanent, in spiritual terms.

The poet Longfellow put this point well in his lines,

> *"Not in the clamour of the crowded street*
> *Nor in the shouts and plaudits of the throng*
> *But in ourselves, are triumph and defeat"*

We can usually trace our ancestry back several generations. Some take pride in their genealogy, claiming to be descendants of someone famous or important in history. Genetically they may be accurate, but spiritually we must look at each incarnation as standing alone. Our parents are not our parents, and our children are not our children spiritually. In restating this, it is not my intention to undermine the joy and value of family relationships. They have an important place in the overall journey of experiencing what love is and what it is not, as some of my own lives show.

Our spiritual lineage only has the relationship with our Thirds as a thread to unite our many varied past lives. The following timeline summarises my past lives, but not the spiritual reasoning behind the major events. This I do in the next chapter.

Angie	Roger	Tay	Notes on Life
	7994-7962BC Neolithic	Brother	Lived in the area since known as Jericho
2302-2254BC Amhika Worker of cotton cloth		2310-2244BC Tshoka – Husband Labourer in granary	Area was Mohenjo Daro near River Indus now known as Pakistan
1704-1671BC Kia (Ankhesenisis) – Sister Handmaiden in temple of Isis		1706-1682BC Tjelamunra – Brother Priest in temple of Ra	Present life friend Ann was Meritra
1528-1484BC Tyche Lady of the night. Stabbed by client	1524-1470BC Philon Sailor in Minoan civilisation, now Crete		
	1046-1004BC Abisha Scribe in Hebrew city of Har Megiddo	Died 1004BC Abijah – Brother Potter	Har Megiddo is on the Nahal Iron pass. It was hit by earthquake. Both died
Raka – Wife	926-873BC Bahska Nubian in Napata, Kush		Present life son Harry was the son who worked in household of Shabaka the ruler

	810-744BC Eudamidas Phoenician ship owner	782-766BC Daughter
	638-589BC Acreisus Sculptor in Cortina, Etrusca. Studied under Sopatros	624-560BC Theotimos Student of Acreisus Mother in present life was fellow student under Sopatros named Gaios
47BC-AD01 Sister	50BC-AD10 Historian Other planet	
1249-73 Jeh – Wife	1247-90 Fet Ipicas tribe, Brazil	Bonded in 1262 5 children
1299-1358 Alba – Mother	1318-40 Ansel Poitiers, France. Battle of Sluys	Served under Barbnoir and Quriel. Killed in sea battle
1482-90 Sister	1480-96 Namdev India, Mogul empire	

1539-97 Anne Roper – Wife	1537-1603 Thomas Roper Scribe to cloth merchant	Married April 1559 4 children knew of William Shakespeare
	1628-95 Enku Japanese priest, sculpting Buddha	Dai Assistant and novice Vowed to make 120,000 images of Buddha
	Aug 1735-Sept 1781 Tobias Furneaux Sea captain of ship Adventure, 1771 Pacific	James Tobias Swilley Servant Born Swilley near Portsmouth, lived in Devon and Cornwall
	1853-73 Sean O'brien White Star Line ship Atlantic	1842-73 Liam O'brien – Brother Sank off Nova Scotia 1873, 547 killed
	1890-1917 Peter Crawford Lance Corporal. Royal Sussex Regiment. Was a volunteer. Died in Flanders at the Hindenberg line	1884-1916 George Taylor Sergeant. Died battle of Somme Father was Jack, killed at sea in 1915 on HMS Viknor

Please note: with the one exception these are incarnations on Earth only. Tay has incarnated with Angie since 1682BC, just not here.

CHAPTER THREE

DISCUSSION BASED ON CASE STUDY

William Shakespeare probably went as far as he could with the message *"And one man in his time plays many parts"*. For him to write of reincarnation, to further define "time" and to explain the "many parts" as the experiencing of the many facets of "love", would have perhaps courted a heresy charge. His psychotherapy, to use modern idiom, was pointing out that the parts in life we each play are only roles, not our real being, our true spiritual nature.

One point I have not made clear is that the lives I have described are those of my later spiritual career. My own spiritual childhood would not have been on Earth, but a planet that was the nursery world before Earth had that status. I previously related that older spirits need incarnations on Earth, as it offers the unique opportunity for certain experiences available only here. Life here is a challenge for everyone, and particularly so for the older spirits. I have heard Earth described as "the planet of emotions". Perhaps more accurately, it is the planet of the negative emotions, as these are more powerfully prevalent than the positive ones.

REASONS WHY

Before going further with additional material, it would be salutary to make a list of some of the important spiritual experiences from my past lives. Being the distillation of fourteen lives spread over four millennia, this must be a rather unique teaching aid! In doing so, I hope to achieve the aim of the book, which was to explain why we return to human form. At the very least, I hope to give an insight into the spiritual reasoning for my experiencing certain events in my lives, which may in turn, help the reader to obtain a different perspective, and so understand events in their own current life from a spiritual point of view.

In my personal case, therefore, why I returned to human form was to experience the following spiritual lessons:

- Others' expectations of one should not influence your behaviour.
- You, and only you, are the shaper of your destiny.
- In a spiritual culture, the lesson can be the denial of self and the moving into the spiritual while in the physical.
- One should look beyond the outward physical appearance and search for the inner spiritual beauty.
- No amount of physical riches can purchase peace for the soul.
- Wealth and power have illusory value, being solely of the physical and nothing else.
- One aim of terminal illness can be to come to a state of peace about departure from the physical.
- The giving and sharing of one's talents in an open way is the spiritual way, not in a resentful way, fearful of being outshone.
- Love can, in certain circumstances, be standing in for a person where they themselves are unable to complete a role.
- One can feel different love for different people within one's life. Feeling love for one person does not necessarily prohibit feelings for another or lessen their value.
- It matters not what men say with their lips, it is what they know and believe in their spirit that really matters.
- Spiritual enlightenment and advancement is not to be gained by following another's way, but by finding the way for oneself.
- The pursuit of any goal that has as its reason only satisfaction or glorification of self is not the way to achieve growth of spirit.
- One chooses one's own path; one human cannot be accountable for the experiences of another.
- Enforcing what you believe to be good for others, can in certain circumstances be the correct course of action, where

- they themselves are not in full possession of the facts or cannot make an informed decision.
- ❖ Contrast is a great teacher.
- ❖ Biological relationship does not necessarily mean love or even liking.
- ❖ Love can sometimes be leading a person to his destiny, even where that destiny is tragic in earthly terms.
- ❖ Spiritual growth comes from learning to forgive and accept others with their faults, realising that they are spiritual beings, and the faults are only an earthly manifestation.
- ❖ A relationship with a parent can be biological only; sometimes it can be intentionally chosen for the lack of spiritual compatibility in order to demonstrate that same point.
- ❖ Love can sometimes be the recognition of your spiritual one third at some depth of your being.
- ❖ War has a spiritual value in the heightened and varied emotions that can be experienced through it.

The spiritual concepts I have summarised are not conventional wisdom, and are open to criticism in many cases. As with the whole concept of the spiritual, my reply is, does it have the ring of truth to it? Does it offer a rational explanation to experiences where otherwise none might exist? I have no wish to preach or attempt to convert anyone, only to enlighten and to foster spiritual understanding in those who seek it.

I had some questions to put to our guide about two of my lives, which I document next.

FIRST WORLD WAR EXPERIENCE

Along with many others, I was a volunteer. My first question on this life was, "As an older spirit, why did I take part instead of being an objector?" Our guide replied that older spirits are not saints; they are just highly evolved spirits seeking to complete their experiences. For all spirit, young and old, the correct course of action is to do whatever it is necessary for you to do, in order to achieve the experiences you are attempting to cover in the plan for that life. If the plan is that you be an objector, then be an objector and learn the lessons that brings.

If the plan is that you take part and learn by so doing, then it is not incorrect to become a member of the fighting forces. Remember, masters are truly enlightened spirits, what you would call saints, and one would not expect them to fight a war, but even older spirits such as those of level five, are still completing their experiences. What is correct or incorrect for each individual in any circumstance, is what is determined by their particular life-plan for the incarnation.

The historian John Keegan in his book, "The First World War" wrote, *"Men whom the trenches cast into intimacy entered into bonds of mutual dependency and sacrifice of self stronger than any of the friendships made in peace and better times. That is the ultimate mystery of the First World War. If we could understand its loves, as well as its hates, we would be nearer to understanding the mystery of human life".*

John Keegan has come close, possibly without realising it, to the spiritual reasoning for the war as it affects the individual. On a planetary level, a further degree of explanation would attribute the war to a lesson for the civilised West that it had gone too far away from spirituality.

My second question therefore, concerned the war itself; "Why was it necessary?"

Our guide answered: *"War is, I am sorry to say, necessary on your planet until it reaches a certain stage of evolution. When a soul chooses to incarnate on Earth, it knows it is going to be using the tools of the human race; knows it will be subject to the human lack of spiritual understanding and evolution; subject to the human characteristics passed genetically. It brings its own essence and the task is to realise itself in the surroundings it has chosen.*

Earth however, needs to progress in its own way, needs to advance, and the human race needs to raise its vibration. This is what happens in all worlds, until they are no longer nursery worlds. It is only by realising one's own nature that one can set about changing it, and in a war all the emotions I described are magnified, concentrated, because of the events raging around them. A soul incarnated into a war experiences a greater range of emotion in a shorter space of time than usual. Their experience in the incarnation is greater for the experience of war."

Why Come Back? Book 2

Our guide continued, *"What is planned is that eventually man will accept and acknowledge the spiritual way, will no longer need to have these injections of experience to raise his vibration. This is beginning; the new cycle is seeing an increase in spiritual awareness already, even though it is in its infancy.*

Do not forget, every plan you make for yourself has at its core the need to advance spiritually. Earth needs its incarnated souls to gain spiritual enlightenment while in the physical so that Earth itself can become more spiritual and so advance from its role as a nursery. The needs of the two can be met by their interaction, just as the needs of spirit Threes can be met by interaction with other spirit Threes."

At the time of drafting the manuscript, September 2001, there was in the world news, the terrorist attacks on the World Trade Centre. It seemed from the media that there was a majority call for retaliation and retribution (mostly masculine). A small minority voice however (mostly female), called for peace and harmony. The great task is to reverse these proportions and without gender bias.

Many have noticed the culture of the Wild West Marshall in the USA's language and actions following September 11th. What a contrast can be observed between this, and the Dalai Lama's reaction to the invasion of Tibet and subsequent murder of one million Tibetans. (Man's propensity for aggression and brutality and the constant warfare in the world, has occupied my thoughts greatly. I return to the subject and its further spiritual explanation in the next book.)

Another point from the First World War life is the recognition of one's third in the lifetime. Step one is to do this on an unconscious level, and step two is to understand the spiritual connection. I asked why the task occurs more than once.

Our guide replied by saying that the task of recognition of the other third is repeated often throughout the levels. It is one of those that reoccur even if you do get it right in an incarnation. What happens is that each time it occurs and is met, the feeling becomes stronger until the incarnation in which there is full realisation whilst still in the incarnated state. It goes without saying of course, that this is only the case on Earth and other worlds when at nursery level, as more evolved societies know about spiritual connection in their incarnated state; it is a basic knowledge to them.

To be brought to the full realisation whilst incarnated on Earth, is a task given only to the higher level five spirits. This would lead me, our guide continued, when I thought it through, to realise that all higher level five spirit must incarnate here or on another nursery world to attain this step of progression, if this knowledge is known elsewhere. Indeed he said, you cannot achieve that particular task in a world where the knowledge is commonplace, but there are other tasks in those worlds that achieve for the soul the same benefit as this one does on Earth.

SEA CAPTAIN, THE JAMES COOK PERIOD

The point about meeting of thirds can be further illustrated here and a subtle difference revealed. I questioned how this differed from the Peter Crawford example, where there was recognition of the third. Surely in this seafaring life it must have happened at the subconscious level?

Our guide replied, *"In this life, Tobias showed kindness to me, his slave, due to his nature and spirituality, rather than due to the fact that he had recognised me as his third. He felt drawn to me and I to him and the friendship that grew from that was important to us both without our knowing why. It was a connection that formed from the kindness and friendship shown".* In the case of Peter and George, the connection was recognised. They felt the contact of their spirits, again not understanding why, but in this case the friendship formed out of the connection recognised although not understood.

By way of further information, Tobias Furneaux was first lieutenant aboard "HMS Dolphin" on his first circumnavigation. What history does not record is how the meeting between Tobias and his slave took place, so I asked him! Our guide replied, *"I joined him during his voyage aboard the Dolphin, he purchased me from a slaver he saw beating me. I would undoubtedly have died had he not intervened."*

In summarising this life, our guide had made no mention of the feats of sailing as being of value spiritually. "Is that the case?"

I asked, "Could one generalise and say much of what is regarded as human achievement is not so from a spiritual perspective?"

He replied saying that it is fair to say that much of what is regarded as human achievement is not so from a spiritual perspective, but asked me to note the word **much**. He explained the spiritual value of gaining a professional qualification in the face of indifference and without support, a sub-plot in my current life-plan. That achievement has spiritual implications for me, but not major ones. He went on to say that this can be the case, and indeed was so for Tobias. To be the first European to circumnavigate the globe in both directions was a notable achievement, and one in which he learned to be appreciative of himself, rather than disparaging of his own achievements.

In the present day (and at the time it happened apparently), I was having difficulty with the point about the diet and the freewill lesson. "Was there a failure on my part to explain the reasons for the recommended diet to the seamen?" I queried, "Should such an explanation have accompanied the freedom to choose I allowed them?"

Our guide replied that it was expected of me, as commander of the ship to force my crew to follow Cook's instructions and eat the sauerkraut that would prevent scurvy. Our guide continued by saying that I, Tobias, was already by that time on a spiritual path and had knowledge of freewill choice. I believed that by forcing the crew to eat the sauerkraut I was denying them this freewill choice. What I had failed to realise was that although freewill choice should operate in matters large and small, there should be sufficient information given to those who are to make the choice so that it is an informed one. In some cases, where the persons concerned do not have sufficient intelligence to make an informed choice, it may be the freewill choice of the commander or leader to make that choice for them and for their own good.

Our guide wished to make the point that throughout our history, much falsehood, much cruelty and barbarity has been committed under the guise of what is good for others, and this is not what is condoned here. There is a world of difference between teaching others to eat a diet to promote their health, a diet that due to choice of birth and education you know is correct, and by choice of birth and education, they do not, and for instance, foisting a religion on them that they do not want, when they do have views of their own on the matter.

Our guide wished further to make the point, that if, once you are sure they understand the reasoning, that they are in possession of the facts and have sufficient intelligence to make an informed decision, they still choose to ignore the information, then that of course is their freewill choice and may be accepted as such. As Tobias, it appears I was well on the way to correct spiritual thinking, but I mistakenly thought it correct to allow the crew freewill choice in a matter which affected their health; a matter in which they did not possess either the facts or sufficient intelligence to appreciate the facts had they been privy to them.

In this situation, continued our guide, if I wished to allow the crew freewill choice and had difficulty in imposing my will on them in this matter, I should at least have made sure they were in full possession of the facts and demonstrated the correct choice by making it myself and eating the prescribed diet.

One can see a parallel here in modern politics. A government may prescribe a vaccination policy, for example, but its leaders may not lead by example with their own children, or may refuse to comment on their personal lives when pressed, as is the case at the time of writing, of the British Prime Minister, Tony Blair, when questioned about whether his own baby son had been vaccinated.

I wish to leave my individual past lives now, and look at two broader spiritual topics, those of soul groups and freewill.

SOUL GROUPS

I discussed in *"Why Come Back?"* the expression "soul groups". By "soul group" our guide meant only to indicate that there is an association in more than one lifetime with a spirit, other than one's third. The term seemed appropriate as a means of explanation.

Our guide realised in some of the publications we have read, and possibly the reader too, the term is used to indicate a group of souls that you rejoin on return to spirit, but this is not exactly what he means to convey in his usage of it. Some writers have suggested there are pools of souls from which fellow players are selected in planning a life and that these groups join up again on return to spirit. This is not exactly correct. You will have souls that you have worked with before but these souls may or may not have ever worked with each other. It may be that they have all appeared in differing lives or in different aspects of the same life with you, and never have encountered each other. In this way they are not really a group, which infers that they would all be together and known to each other.

A better way of viewing them would be as your own personal soul address book. Just as in an earthly address book, you would know all the persons represented; some would know each other, and some would know only you. From this familiar collection of souls you may decide to choose your fellow players.

To elaborate, our guide explained that not all players in your play have to come from this collection, not even all major ones, but they can do and it is quite likely that they will. Note the point, it is **quite likely** that your major players will come from the collection of souls with whom you are familiar, having shared past incarnation, but it is **not essential** that they do. It could be that one of your major players is a complete unknown, sharing a first incarnation with you.

Furthermore, our guide advised the only thing that is, to use my phrase, "set in stone" about the format on your return to spirit, is that you will join with your other two thirds and review your life-plan with them. You may meet with others from your familiar collection who were involved in the life to compare notes; you may even have the input from those of the collection who did not accompany you this time; these souls may have an interest in your development because they have shared lives with you previously. You may do these things, or just as possibly, you may not. You may just be involved in terms of life review, with your own two thirds and no others.

For ease of explanation, our guide gave us the analogy of a director casting a group of actors for a play; the director, presented with actors unknown to his star or with actors he knows have worked successfully with his star performer before, the familiar would be chosen if at all possible. There may be lifetimes where many appear whom one has "worked with" previously. In contrast there may be lifetimes where the only repeat encounter is with one's third.

The examples of known players in my current life are: my mother, who was once a fellow student; my son in this life, who has been our joint son previously; Angela's son, who was our joint son previously; my brother, who has been our joint son; Angela's friend in this life has also been a friend in a past life. (I referred in book one to telepathic communication ability that these two have in times of heightened emotion).

You may wish to see one of the souls that has been a key person in your life, your mother, spouse, sibling or so on, although this is more usual in younger spirit, who may seek the familiar on return to their natural spirit state. That is, until they understand sufficiently that the spirit state is the familiar and the incarnated state the unfamiliar. If this person you wish to see is your other third, then it is quite definite that you will see them again. If they are one of the familiar souls, or even one that you are interacting with for the first time, then it may be possible to see them, but they may have an agenda of their own to pursue, or be of a spiritual age different to yours, which would make it difficult for such a meeting to take place. In any event, it has to be desirous to both parties.

Time spent in spirit may include time spent in assisting those incarnated with whom you have connection; time spent serving as tutor or adviser to younger spirit; time spent helping to write and review life-plans with younger spirit, provided of course, you are of sufficient spiritual age to be called upon to do this; time spent assisting those of your cluster on their return to spirit; but predominantly it will be time spent with your other two thirds, reviewing this last and all other lives, assimilating information, planning, casting for the next life, and growing together.

In summary, our guide repeated that the whole purpose of incarnation, is to come to an understanding, whilst incarnated, of that which all know when in spirit; to work through the various experiences required to enrich your soul and in turn your Three and again in turn, the Collective. I feel, at the risk of belabouring the point, that it may be beneficial to reiterate this answer, in the hope of clearing any confusion. The only ones who actually form a group that you can be **positive** of being with on return to spirit and of incarnating with again in future lives, are the other two elements of your own Three. This is the only certainty.

You may, however, find yourself incarnating on a regular basis with other souls who you have worked with before and with whom you have a familiarity. Older spirits, who have incarnated many times, will have accrued a nucleus of "preferred souls" with whom to work. Even then it is still possible to choose an incarnation in which there are no familiar souls at all; to go through a life meeting only souls with which they have no previous connection except for their own third. This may never happen, but for some it can. What is more likely, is that the preferred actors will be the ones chosen to play the roles of key figures in the lifetime, and in turn of course, you will be playing the role of a key figure in their lifetime.

FREEWILL

I would like to revisit the topic of freewill and life-plans. I explained in *"Why Come Back?"* that freewill was really the opportunity to make a decision from choices, not pure freewill. I wondered further, how does freewill relate to life-plans, particularly in the context of the statement, "events can fail to take place that are planned, but nothing takes place that is not planned", even if that planning is rapid rescripting by the guide?

Our guide replied that the importance is all in the wording and earthly languages can be so restrictive. The point is, he recapped, in matters of freewill it is possible to make, what we will call an incorrect choice; this means a choice which delays following the true path of your journey for the incarnation, or even going off the path altogether. It does not mean that a plan is not in place for this eventuality.

To elaborate, freewill is a choice between alternatives, and a plan is in place for each of those alternatives, but only one will be the correct choice, which leads you without falter in pursuit of your goal. When I have spoken of a guide needing to do some rapid rescripting because an incorrect choice has been made, this refers to the guide bringing into the script, setting in motion, the plan for the eventuality of the wrong choice being made. In minor matters, of course, a guide has daily scripting authority.

I am personally aware of two instances where I took a major decision that was not in my plan. These were my decision to take up employment in a foreign country and the purchase of a much larger house when I had been back in the UK for a period. Our guide advised *"Rather than say life events not planned, it would be correct to say life events where the correct choice was not made. You have said yourself that freewill is really a choice of alternatives. In the two scenarios you mention, you chose the wrong alternative. This does not mean that we had not planned what would happen if you made that choice, just that it was not the best one to make".*

Our guide confirmed that this is the case in all matters of freewill. The plan will be made for the correct choice, the choice that leads one on to further development. Certain "actors" will be cast before incarnation and the guide will cast others at the appropriate time. Plans will also be made for the contingency of choosing an incorrect choice. The guide may need to rescript minor details as the incarnation progresses, remember, the statement "events can fail to take place that are planned, but nothing that takes pace without planning" refers to major events in a life, not the trivia.

In many cases it will be so planned that, although by making an incorrect choice and missing one objective of your planned journey, the incorrect choice may lead one back to the path by a circuitous route. A sidetrack that means that the true journey is delayed, but still arrived at. Some, of course, result in complete failure and some mean the missing of one objective, the intended one, but completion of another.

It is also true that, although younger spirit has fewer things to achieve in a life than does older spirit, for some, particularly the extreme beginners, little is left to chance and more of the detail is determined before incarnation, to give them better possibility of achieving the little that is expected. This is not the same for older spirit. The challenge is, for all the thirds, even the guide, to sort out more of it as the life goes on, bringing in the alternatives to give the chance again of making a correct decision where the alternatives planned may lead one completely off track!

However, even in beginner lives, freewill does operate and the incarnated one can make choices, which means the planned detail does not occur. As noted, if a wrong alternative is chosen, there will be an alternative in place, but the guide may need to do some rescripting.

We had an enquirer who wished to have knowledge of job change, house move and number of children. I raised a point about the amount of detail given, and was told that this can be due to yet another reason to any of the points noted above. Our guide explained, *"When spirit allows this degree of information to be passed, it can be because choices have already been made and scripting has already been put in place, which means that these events will come to pass. Even though the enquirer may be unaware of it, they have made the choices that have started the chain of events that will lead to this.*

In the case to which you refer, it is because of a combination of these. In two of the points you mention, choices have already been made which will lead to this and the scripting has been done already. In the third point, the spirit is young and this detail has been pre-planned. Even though freewill can still operate, all the alternatives will lead, eventually, back to the same result."

The age of a spirit has a relationship to the amount of detail that goes into a life-plan. The guide scripts in daily "trivia" and also may be called on to script in the alternative "pre-arranged" plan when a choice is made through freewill, which was not the choice hoped for at the outset of the life.

The life-plan is often written in such a way that the crossroads points are difficult to spot at the time of their occurrence. For example, those that have seen the 1998 film *"Titanic"* may recall the card game scene at the beginning, where New World hopefuls play to kill time before the boat sails. One man bets his ticket and loses it to another, who then goes in his place. What a reversal in destinies, you might think! But no, the man who did not go may have been just as deeply affected by his "lucky escape" and his life-plan so achieved, as the man who did go, whose destiny was to do so but who did not know it until the ship was about to depart! The sinking of the *"Titanic"*, pronounced unsinkable but doing so on her maiden voyage, has captured the interest of subsequent generations, and will continue to do so. It provides an illustration of life-plan in many ways in the lives of the various participants.

The ease with which a destiny can be unknowingly defeated by freewill choice can be illustrated in my own case. I more than once, had seriously contemplated emigration with my family. That caused some concern for my guide! Secondly, once I had been forcibly relieved by our divorce laws of parental responsibility, I set out to achieve a long-held ambition to world cruise on a yacht. In both scenarios, had I not stayed in Lincolnshire, England, I would have failed to meet Angela, and thus caused my life-plan failure.

It is not always permissible that one knows the major plot for an incarnation, or indeed, even the minor ones. If these were known, where would be the growth when one came to a crossroads choice? One would know without doubt, which route to take and so be denied the growth that the choice occasions.

In spirit, one plans things that will lead to growth. The things planned may be painful to experience in the incarnated state, physically or emotionally painful, but can actually be a success in spiritual terms because of what they teach. For instance, a bad marriage can lead to much heartache for the participants; they can view its eventual end as a failure. In fact, in spiritual terms, it can have represented a huge success because of the growth, the knowledge of self, and ultimately, the knowledge of love gained from the experience. Do not forget that a negative teaches, by very comparison, the nature of the positive.

In communication with one's guide, there are limits to what may be said so as not to interfere with freewill choice, although they can, and do, drop hints. When asked by their incarnated thirds, if it is correct to do a certain thing in their lives, spirit guides can only answer spiritually, that it is correct or not correct to do this. They cannot forewarn you that in doing something you will bring pain and distress upon yourself or others, as if they were to do so, you would most likely avoid the path and in so doing fail to learn the lesson that the event is intended to teach.

In summary, even though prior to incarnation you made a plan for your life, during the incarnation all have freewill choice at certain major crossroads. Failure to negotiate a crossroads correctly is what leads to a need to repeat an incarnation in order to try again to discover the lesson offered by the choice. In every incarnation on Earth, a spirit has an agenda that includes one major plot for the life and several minor plots. Failure in the major plot will almost certainly demand a repeat life; failure in a minor one will not always necessarily do so, as it may be incorporated in a future life containing a new major plot. I hope you can see how even an apparent wrong choice can lead back to the correct path, although delaying things in the process, that freewill choice operates, but it is still true to say "that events can fail to take place that are planned, but nothing takes place without planning".

CHAPTER FOUR

OUR CURRENT LIVES UNDER THE MICROSCOPE

At times in my life, before my spiritual awakening, I would have quite agreed with Shakespeare's Hamlet *"How flat, stale and unprofitable seem to me the uses of this world"*. Later on in life, having come to agreement with Keats that life is *"the vale of soul-making"*, I would have been lost for any further words to elaborate on that. I trust this chapter will provide the detail that I previously could not and illustrates my statement that life indeed is not what it seems, that we are here to experience love in its many forms.

    We have found a number of people who have sought mediumship from Angela, have current life emotional issues, which have turned the meeting into more of a psychotherapy session from spirit. The reader may relate to some of the sub-plots in my current life and so gain insight into their own experiences, through the spiritual explanation behind them.

    In my first book I offered details of the main events in my current life, and discussed them from the spiritual viewpoint as an example of life-plans and what goes into them, and then I offered a comparison with the actual events. Being an older spirit, my life was never going to be easy! I did not go into detail about the spiritual value of the events and this I now wish to do.

    I asked our guide to confirm the spiritual lessons, the aspects of love experienced, by the main plot and sub-plots of my current incarnation.

    The points listed are the actual words of our guide, our remaining third in spirit. I wish to point out that the spiritual reasoning for the main plots and sub-plots is as it applies to us in this incarnation. They are not necessarily generalised explanations for all levels of spirit for the same experiences.

Again, I wish to emphasise, I use my current life for teaching and illustrative purposes, for the spiritual insights obtainable, not for vanity or self-glory.

MAIN PLOT OF MY LIFE – TO WRITE AND TEACH

The main plot is to write and teach about spirit. At the time of writing, just getting book one published had proved a challenge as all mainstream publishers have rejected it. This main plot is therefore yet to be achieved. The fact that Angela and I should both divorce in 1995 and then met early in the New Millennium was no coincidence. The fact that we have been given this information to publish and that the timing of this coincided with the start of the third millennium is no isolated, individual agenda, but has a part in the greater plan concerning the raising of the spiritual vibration of the planet.

Writing books is not the sole means of bringing people to spirit. Complementary medicine and alternative therapies generally are obvious further examples, for which there is an increasing number of practitioners and acceptance. The reader may recall from my earlier book, teaching is level-five syllabus, when reaching the end of that level. It is not expected of all spirit, only older spirit nearing the end of their journey of experiences.

Our guide gave the following spiritual reasoning:

- ❖ The task is, as a high level spirit, to bring into the public domain information of a level not previously imparted except to a select few, for their own use only.
- ❖ This task will present its own challenges. Your work will not be easily accepted by many, will attract its critics as well as its disciples. You may find yourselves the target of abuse and ridicule by those of lesser spiritual development, and those who fear the change to the established order that the new information could cause.
- ❖ To be able to continue with the task; to be able to deal with the negative in order to reap the positive; to reach out with love to those who do embrace the knowledge you give; to reach out with love also to those who do not embrace the knowledge.

- ❖ To give unstintingly of your time and your experience to those who wish to learn from you.
- ❖ To do all this in the name of love and without ego; without the need of fame, but if fame should befall you, to love yourselves enough to accept it and use it for the further good of others.

SUB-PLOT – DIVORCE AND LOSS OF THE FAMILY UNIT

This proved no small task for me. Loss of daily contact with my children following divorce was most painful. It was compounded by one of my daughters largely refusing to have any communication with me, a situation that still persists.

In *"Why Come Back?"* I discussed the hard-to-believe spiritual truth that we choose our parents. Thus my children chose me as a father. Paternal love is largely unrecognised by our culture, at least, that is my experience of our divorce laws. Separation from one's children, I would describe as a "living bereavement": the loved ones have not died, but the sense of loss is similar.

From the vantage point gained by the passage of time, and by reaching the knowledge I now have, most of this sub-plot has been achieved. I cannot go as far as to offer thanks to my ex-wife for the experience, but knowledge of the spiritual reasoning behind the event has allowed me to let go of much of the bitterness I once felt.

Our guide gave the spiritual explanation for this experience as follows:

- ❖ To learn that children are only yours biologically, to learn that your love therefore is a love of a spiritual entity that just happens to be in a close incarnation to you this time.
- ❖ To realise then, that if one can love these spirit entities that are only close to you by virtue of birth, that have no relationship to you other than a biological one, then one can love all spirit entities.
- ❖ To realise that people are spirits having a human experience and so, if they are spirit entities, you should learn to love them all, just as you do those who have incarnated closely with you.
- ❖ To further learn, while incarnated, of life-plans.

- ❖ To have your love for another used against you; used to hurt until you feel pain and resentment. To then take the huge spiritual step of realising that this was in that person's plan, was in your plan, and that in fact they helped you to achieve your plan which was exactly the coming to this realisation.
- ❖ Having taken this conceptual leap, to let go the hurt and resentment, to forgive and to accept that spirit assisted you and should deserve your thanks rather than your resentment and bitterness.

SUB-PLOT – ACHIEVEMENT IN THE FACE OF OBSTRUCTION

Another difficult one! Although I have now forgiven him, I carried anger inside me for twenty years because of my father's behaviour towards me as a teenager and young adult. It took me that long to grasp the now obvious truism, that holding anger only hurts the sufferer, not the one who caused the suffering. It is therefore pointless, even harmful, preventing one from fully enjoying life until it is learned that forgiveness is the antidote to emotional poisoning.

My lesson was to come to the recognition that he is a younger spirit, which makes him, therefore, not capable of the qualities I expected of him. He was jealous of my intelligence and would have preferred me to leave education at the earliest age, sixteen. His refusal to offer me any financial support was instrumental in my decision not to take up the offer of a university place when aged eighteen. The life-plan was for me to have pursued this course despite his obstruction.

The "achievement" of the sub-plot was obtaining a professional qualification at the age of twenty-one. In later life, I made up for missing university to some extent, by obtaining an Open University degree.

Our guide gave us the following explanation:

- ❖ Again, the connection between you and the obstructing parent in this case, is biological only.

- ❖ This being understood you can realise that you chose your parent in order to experience achievement without support.
- ❖ To be able to love yourself for your achievement; not to feel the human necessity to make light of it, but to glory in it; not with the sort of pride that in its own way begets a feeling of superiority over your fellows, but with a true and open heart; to have a pure joy in achievement for its own sake, not as a means of setting you above others.
- ❖ Further, to see life-plan at work and to realise that your father has fulfilled his and your destiny and so is not deserving of resentment or bitterness.
- ❖ To recognise the attachment is at a biological level only and so not to expect him to have your opinions and views on life. To forgive him this and allow him to be his own person, rather than harbouring a wish that he should be otherwise, this is an awakening of the lesson of love for all.

SUB-PLOT – ILLNESS IN ONE CLOSE TO YOU

The spiritual purpose of a major illness was not in my thoughts when my previous partner suffered a brain tumour and underwent surgery a year later. My instinct at the time was to be the supportive one; to treat her as I would wish to be treated were our places reversed.

It was intended that this sub-plot be achieved through the death at a relatively young age of my mother. She did so die, but I was not greatly affected by her illness, as I was working abroad. Her death, though, did of course affect me deeply. The illness in my partner is an example of "re-scripting" by the guide, not to cause her illness as this would be part of her own life-plan, but to "arrange" that we become partners.

Our guide gave us the following spiritual reasoning for this:

- ❖ Illness in one close to you awakens feelings of inadequacy, of anger against God or even against the sufferer, for being the cause of your unrest.
- ❖ It hammers home man's mortality more that any other event, more even at times, than illness in oneself.

- It presents the greatest opportunities to offer the afflicted one unconditional love, to support them, to assuage their anxieties and to help them to accept the love of others. People of strong and dependable personality perhaps have the hardest time of all accepting the love of others. They can try so hard not to be a burden, that this very fact becomes burdensome! They need to be shown how to accept the care and concern offered to them and how to open to the love around them.
- Contact with one in this situation can teach compassion, gentleness, support and the sharing of strength.
- If one is able to accept the knowledge of life-plans and the knowledge that we are all a part of God, accept that as He is eternal then so all spirit is eternal, then death of loved ones and their illnesses and disabilities can be viewed in a different light. No longer is it necessary to feel bereft, to feel personal grief at their loss or anger at their illness.
- It is possible to see that unconditional love is allowing them to fulfil their destiny and to be accepting of their plan. By doing so, you can experience a leap in perception, which in turn will lead to a leap in progression.

SUB-PLOT – ACCOMPLISHMENT DESPITE BEING TIED TO AN UNSUPPORTIVE PARTNER

My parents believed my choice of bride to be unsuitable but did not voice an opinion. Later, friends sometimes asked, "What do you two have in common?" Physical attraction and the children was the answer. It was a "parent-child" relationship, rather than a relationship shared by two adults, but it worked for nineteen years!

The "accomplishment" referred to here is that I started and ran my own business in 1983. My wife opposed this, saying employment was the safer option. I borrowed money to buy an established business and initially worked long hours to ensure it was a success. I did not ask for any help with the business from my wife, as we had young children, and none was offered. My work was an alien world to my wife and so I was unable to confide business problems to her to much extent when they arose. The business prospered and we were, as a family, able to raise our living standards. Every four years or so, my wife would say she wanted a divorce, which of course, destabilised me until the crisis passed.

You might say "How did you come together then, if it was obvious to other parties you were unsuitably matched?" Just after my divorce, I met a divorced lady whose marriage breakdown had circumstances that paralleled my own. She said she had met her husband at a party and it was love at first sight. She now believed that "love is not only blind, but deaf, dumb and stupid too!" She was like us all, unaware at the time of life-plans and the fact that the partners we choose are written into the script for the experiences they can provide.

So what about the point about the "stupid" decision for an intelligent person? Well, I wondered if Mr Fixit upstairs can temporarily arrange for you to suspend your reasoning faculties, so you in fact, take a decision for "emotional" reasons. The answer is yes, our guides will sometimes "over-ride" our control systems as it were, and by doing so help us achieve our destined experience.

On the other hand, guides can help us out of an experience as well as into one. The meeting of this lady (unlikely as she lived quite a distance from me) at the time when I needed to better understand my marriage breakdown, was an example of "synchronicity" again. Not only did her story show me I was not alone in my experience, she also recommended a certain book, which greatly helped my understanding of certain character types, of which both our respective ex-partners were examples.

Our guide gave the spiritual viewpoint of this experience:

- ❖ The reason for this is similar to that for choosing an unsupportive parent. Achievement made alone provides you with a sense of your own worth.
- ❖ Knowledge of the fact that you can achieve your goals without the need of an emotional prop strengthens your belief in yourself and your own ability. In short, it helps you to learn to love yourself.
- ❖ The other side of this coin is to learn to accept the help and support of another when it is offered. This is equally important and necessary to have a complete understanding

of love. In your case, this is a lesson offered under a different "heading", not under this one.

- A further reason for having an unsupportive partner can be the lesson of learning that the physical attraction that draws you to a partner initially is no substitute for the attraction of like minds.
- That those on the same spiritual vibration as yourself and therefore able to empathise with your hopes and desires are more likely to take your hopes and dreams and make them their own too. It is possibly the best lesson for showing the difference, the divide, between the earthly biological functions of the vessel for the soul you call a body and the spiritual functions of the mind that feeds and nurtures the soul while it is in the body.
- An unsupportive and unsuitable partner can easily fill the role of providing for the bodily needs, they can feed you, provide for your sexual requirement, bear your children, and tend your home. They cannot however reach you intellectually or make important to them those things which are important to you but for which they do not have the comprehension. They may not even try, recognising at some level, the gulf as being too wide to cross.
- A spiritual partner, however, one who has the ability to share on a spiritual level with you, may or may not be able to do all of the earthly things detailed above but will definitely be able to reach you spiritually and intellectually and will have the greatest comprehension of your hopes, desires and goals. They will without doubt support you in these and incorporate them as their own.
- As with most lessons, one side of the coin cannot be fully understood without experience of the other. So in short, you need to experience the unsupportive, unsatisfactory type of relationship to understand and value any other type.
- In your case, you also experienced the love you had for your wife in your early marriage work against you. When you suffer disappointment with the behaviour of someone for whom you do not have love, it is just disappointment. When you suffer disappointment at the behaviour of someone for whom you do have love, it is so much the greater pain. In time this can turn the love to resentment of the one causing

the pain by causing continual disappointment. Facets of your nature that you do not normally display can be brought to the fore due to your frustration caused by your situation. You love this person but do not wish to love them as loving them is the cause of this pain you do not wish to have.

- ❖ Eventually, as in your case, it can occur that the continued unsupportive behaviour, the unreasonable attitude, can drive you away. You are left so confused and embittered that the love turns, if not to hate, to something resembling it.
- ❖ This is a lesson to be learned, not to let the loss of a love ruin your life and your capacity to love again. Not to allow the joy experienced while the relationship was good, to be lost completely because it is no more. To step away without regret, to allow the other partner to be what it is they have become and to continue to be yourself, not to be altered by their change if you do not wish to be.

SUB-PLOT – PROBLEMS IN BUSINESS VENTURES

I have met many who devote their energies to the accumulation of money, who see that as an end in itself (as I once did), not a means to an end. Also, I have seen people who put, in my phrase, their wallet before their integrity. I have experienced my hand being bitten subsequently, by those I have helped in their careers.

I was, more that once, on the receiving end of legal claims from those who failed to take personal responsibility for their actions, and in so doing, sought redress from me, their professional adviser, merely because I carried insurance, not for any wrong advice on my part. Yes, quite enough problems to make me search for the exit, to seek tranquil waters after a troubled sea!

We were given the following spiritual explanation from our guide:

- ❖ As you know, it was in your plan to run your own business, to keep it until this time to provide the means for you to undertake your current venture. Whatever the outcome following your departure from it, it has served this purpose

and has enabled you to consider embarking on your spiritual odyssey before the normal age of retirement.
- ❖ However, had things run smoothly at all times, the urge to be free, to free the soul and progress on a spiritual level may not have become as strong in you as it has. Had you had a smooth ride, problem free, you may have been happy to join the ranks of the retired businessmen with their cosy lives. This is not meant to deride those who have this, it is possibly not their time to experience anything else and that lifestyle can provide its own lessons on return to spirit if not while in the physical.
- ❖ In your case, however, it was necessary to have sufficient troubles in your life and to facilitate the start of the search for meaning, to provide the yearning for release and freedom for the soul.
- ❖ Additionally, you learned much about human nature in the process, which has also aided you for your future works.

SUB-PLOT – INSINCERITY IN OTHERS

My experience of encountering such people in my life, was given the following explanation, and these are my guide's words (honestly)!:

- ❖ Learning about human nature was a vital part of your progression. It better aids you to identify the spiritual from the physical.
- ❖ It has given you this unique gift of being able to quite quickly sum up a person's spiritual level by example that all are not as sincere and trustworthy as you are yourself.
- ❖ In short, it has prepared you for your current task by teaching the negative side of the human personality.

SUB-PLOT – LOSS OF A SIBLING

My brother Eddie died in a road traffic accident. He was driving alone and no other vehicle was involved. My sister-in-law was devastated and five years after the event, her health is still seriously affected.

My father did not appear to grieve much for the loss of a son as far as I could tell. He said three words only to me at the funeral, and spent his time there with my ex-wife. Later, when I saw him it seemed to me that he expressed pity for himself rather than grief for my brother. He also sought, quite irrationally, to blame the accident on my sister-in-law, rather than support her, as she needed. This of course, only added to her anguish.

Our guide explained the grief I experienced as follows:

- This event provided the experience of the sudden and unexpected loss of one for whom you had affection.
- The love you had for your brother was yet a different kind of love. Not the same as for your mother or your wife or children, but nevertheless, love. Love for one who was related to you by blood and who had shared good and bad times in your life with you. One who had suffered the loss of a mother and the insensitivity of a father with you.
- This love you had for your brother was felt more acutely by its loss as is often the way. You had love for him but realised this more when he was taken away from you. This provided yet a different aspect of love from which to learn.
- You also witnessed the effect Eddie's loss had on your sister-in-law; saw first hand her debilitating grief. You have seen your efforts to support and maintain contact with your sister-in-law bear fruit in the unexpected spiritual growth she has shown recently on your visit.
- You will have the opportunity to work with her spiritually and so learn more of the nature of the love shared by her and Eddie which was the stronger for not being shared with children and strengthened even more because of their shared unhappiness over the lack of children.
- The main lessons from this event were learned by your observation and analysis of the devastating effect of Eddie's loss on his wife and the minimal effect of it on your father as much as the direct effect on you personally.

SUB-PLOT – THWARTED AMBITIONS

Ever since a teenager, I have had a "sail-away" dream; a desire to own my own boat and have the freedom to travel. This had to wait until my late forties. I certainly know the full meaning of "delayed gratification".

This teenage dream is an example of unconsciously tapping into a life-plan, but without knowing the timing, as I do now have a boat. Secondly, it was, unbeknown to me at the time, tapping into past life memories, as I have had occupations connected with the sea in several past lives as the reader now knows.

Our guide gave the spiritual explanation for this:

- ❖ This served two purposes in your plan. First, it would have been "inconvenient", had you departed for a life afloat too soon. You would have missed meeting your third and so achieving the main part of your plan. The sailing away together to work for spirit, or at least, leaving all behind to go away together in some form or another and work for spirit, was always part of your plan. Your having ambitions to sail away for all those years made it more likely that the two of you would make the correct choices when the time came.
- ❖ On the other hand, from a lesson point of view, following a dream, holding fast to an ideal, having ambition in your life, all present numerous occasions to learn about the nature of love. Each of these involves a kind of love in its own right. Then there are the scenarios for some, where they are forced to choose between their dream and something or someone else that they hold dear. To some extent, you did this and chose to remain and be the husband and father till such time that it was not necessary for you to do so, till circumstances released you from your obligations. All these are lessons about the many facets of love.

I now turn to look at some of the sub-plots in the life of my partner Angela. I would ask the reader to keep in mind that not everyone must experience all of these lessons in their own current incarnation, but they are part of the syllabus that all spirit strives to complete eventually. The "props" used to learn each lesson may differ, but the aspect of love is part of the multi-faceted knowledge all spirit incarnates to experience.

(Angie is referred to as "sister" as shorthand for the spiritual connection of being thirds).

SUB-PLOT – DIFFICULTIES THROUGHOUT MARRIED LIFE

There is a whole mini-industry devoted to relationship counselling, with many useful insights. Few perhaps, consider a spiritual perspective. Personal relationships are the crucible, the arena, the mechanism for being and experiencing so much. They are the opportunities to bring out the best and the worst in us, for our greatest joys and our deepest sorrows.

The reason behind all relationships is to evolve our souls. I commented in my first book, that the success of an unhappy marriage is not in lamenting its failure, but realising why it has occurred. Terribly difficult to do this at the time! Caught in a storm, one rushes for shelter, or at least, battens down the hatches, rather than study meteorology! Creatures of emotion, our personal relationships are often governed by those forces, which at times dominate our rational selves. If not in the lifetime, then learning would of course occur in the life-review on return to spirit. What we may feel to be a failure in earthly terms can be the opposite in spiritual ones.

Our guide spoke through Angela to give me this explanation:

- ❖ Of all the sub-plots in her life, this one possibly provided the greatest amount of tuition for our sister. Many of the lessons were learned by observation. Here was a man who loved her; she did not doubt that, even towards the end of the marriage when she believed he was having extra-marital affairs, she still believed that in his way he loved her.
- ❖ She found his love to be controlling and possessive. This did not create a healthy nurturing and mutually fulfilling relationship for them.

- ❖ She possessed sufficient intelligence to know what was happening; to watch with a kind of detachment as her confidence, her will, her personality and her opinions were destroyed and her thoughts controlled.
- ❖ She loved him deeply for many of the earlier years of their relationship, but experienced this love turning more to loyalty, even to dependence.
- ❖ She suffered heartbreak over their differences in opinion concerning the raising of their children and his distance from family life.
- ❖ She reached the point of believing that she was to blame for every ill that befell the family.
- ❖ She worked herself beyond all reasonable expectation as compensation for her imagined failures, juggling home, children and work. Long days were the norm. An unhealthy, unnecessary and ultimately unsatisfactory and unsustainable situation for all parties.
- ❖ Through it all, though, she believed deep down within her, that he could not help the things that she viewed as wrong with the relationship; that it must be "meant to be this way", and even when she took the decision finally to leave, felt disloyal because of it. She compensated for this feeling of disloyalty by taking as little as possible in her divorce.
- ❖ A lesson in love for all concerned; what it should be and what it should not, but there were many lessons here, not just this.

SUB-PLOT – LOSS OF A PARENT AT A YOUNG AGE

We both lost our respective mothers to illness in the same year, 1980, when we were both in our twenties. In each case, this was the parent we held in the higher regard, or with whom we had the closest understanding. We both noticed by its absence, the help from a grandmother that would have been enthusiastically offered, in raising the children of our respective marriages.

Spirit teaches us often that in order to know hot, we must know cold, the yin and yang, that absence of mother love can teach what it is through comparison with it when experienced.

The reference to a "difference in spiritual level" in dealing with bereavement refers to a trial we both shared in our respective fathers, who were best able to deal with the loss by removal or destruction of all our respective mothers' personal effects, including photographs, from the family home. I, too, found this most upsetting behaviour at the time.

Our guide gave this explanation for the experience:

- ❖ This is a plot you share in common, much like your difficult marriages. Our sister was extremely close to her mother; bore her a love that deepened even more because of the support she received from her. This made the blow of her loss even greater when it came.
- ❖ Being an only child with her only living relatives now her father and paternal grandparents, she was left, a young wife with two babies and no family support other than that given by her grandparents.
- ❖ Her father had such difficulty with her mother's death that he sought to obliterate all trace from his home and his life, something our sister had trouble understanding.
- ❖ From all of this a relationship with her grandparents was forged that might otherwise not have been quite as strong as it was.
- ❖ Many lessons again in the one situation. Loss of a loved one, her father's means of dealing with it compared to her own, again a difference in spiritual level illustrated.
- ❖ The deepening of another affection caused by removal of the first, the difference between these two forms of love and the reasons for them. Love of a child for a mother and a deeper than previously love for the grandparents born initially of gratitude.
- ❖ Realisation of the things that her mother would have done to help her, done automatically without a second thought because of their love for each other.
- ❖ Realisation that following the loss of her mother, no one else would do these things – an illustration of mother love.

SUB-PLOT – ESTRANGEMENT FROM A PARENT

A lesson in how love can cause its own pain by one's use of it and interaction with it. Her husband and her father initially enjoyed good relations and shared some common interests, visits being made to each home. Following the disagreement, there was an eight-year period of no contact at all. Sadly though, although contact has been restored with her father, he still keeps quite distant from his daughter and has no contact with grandchildren, and now also great grandchildren. Angela's grandfather spoke to her from spirit about her father, and in his phrase, he is *"still a baby"* spiritually, but he has shown progression in this lifetime in other aspects of his life.

Our guide explained Angela's experience thus:

- ❖ Being an only child, never having to doubt her mother's love, which was displayed as openly as our sister displays her love, she always believed herself loved in the same way by her father. She just assumed the difference in his showing of it was due to the difference in people, the difference between male and female, mother and father. She was made aware of the problems he had with her mother's loss, but again assumed the things he did that she had trouble understanding, were just his way of dealing with his heartbreak and so accepted them.
- ❖ She had always known her father to be a proud and stubborn man, but was hurt to find that his pride was more important to him that she was. He had a disagreement with her husband, which led to a complete severing of contact. Angry words were exchanged between them, and she was left in the difficult position of feeling that her husband would view an attempt by her to contact her father as an act of disloyalty to him. She never for one moment expected that her husband would retract. She did however, believe her father would love her and his grandchildren sufficiently to do so when he had time to reflect and reconsider. Although he was proud and stubborn, she believed he would not let that stand in the way of his love for them. She was wrong.

- ❖ A lesson learned; her father would rather be eaten up by the loss he felt of his daughter and his grandchildren, than retract angry words. She, an older and gentle spirit would never have allowed this situation to continue were she not in such a difficult position. Indeed, just before the end of her marriage, when she no longer felt the need of such loyalty to her husband, she contacted her father and attempted to reunite the family.

SUB-PLOT – MENTAL ILLNESS IN A CHILD

Seeing a child suffer in any way is a lesson that teaches the true nature of mother love more quickly and easily than any other. In Angela's case, her eldest son experienced a complete breakdown in his early twenties when married with a small child and a home to support. Besides caring for the grandchild as often as possible, she assisted in financially supporting the young family to such an extent as to cause herself some degree of financial difficulty.

This received the following spiritual explanation:

- ❖ For a mother to see her child suffer and be unable to do anything to prevent it is perhaps, one of the most heart-rending experiences she is likely to encounter. This, more than any other thing, identifies mother love.
- ❖ To then go further and believe that her failure to correct a situation in the child's early life is the cause of the current suffering, teaches even more about her love. She, whose only wish is to fiercely protect her beloved child, has actually brought about his pain by her failure to act.
- ❖ In our sister's case, she believed her son's condition directly attributable to his early home life. In some, this could have led to bitterness and a wasting of effort in condemnation of things long past on behalf of the beloved child.
- ❖ Fortunately she was able to curb any such negative reactions and concentrate her efforts in support of the child in his time of need rather than waste her energies and her love by regret or by seeking retribution for old wrongs.

SUB-PLOT – ACCIDENT

The accident has been described in my first book. Two years in a wheelchair was a huge experience. Living only on the ground floor of the house created the indignity of not being able to use the bathroom in private. This indignity caused Angela to crawl up the stairs by herself in her attempt to have this degree of self-esteem. She experienced the frustration of some speaking to the one in charge of her wheelchair, rather than to her directly. "How is she today?" not "How are you?" The determination to reduce dependency on drugs and a determination to walk again against medical opinion, were huge achievements of mind over body, and an example of willpower.

Our guide gave us the spiritual reasoning as follows:

- ❖ The motor accident that left Angela disabled was possibly the single most traumatic happening in her life to date.
- ❖ She learned that needing to rely on others is a frightening experience; that working for your family is ultimately easier than seeing them having to work for you.
- ❖ She further learned that her need to support them was her own need, more than theirs.
- ❖ She found that love could be allowing others to love you as well as loving them.
- ❖ She learned the lessons presented by her disability which forever changed her attitude to the disabled, teaching her that their need for dignity should be considered at all times; that disability of the limbs does not signify disability of the intellect as so many seem to believe.
- ❖ She also learned that pain is only affecting of the body; that the mind can control pain, can rise above it.
- ❖ She learned that she, as the injured one, found herself in the role of comforter and supporter to those who suffered grief at her injury or who were embarrassed to be around her because of it.

CONCLUSION

The teachings given here about life events would normally be contained in the life-review undertaken on return to spirit by all spirits. I have been allowed knowledge of them while still incarnated, for illustration purposes. I trust the reader now has a greater insight into the workings of spirit from our case study.

I would repeat, ours are not perhaps typical examples of life-plans, as I think it would be hard to arrive at what constitutes a "typical" life. Prior to incarnation, each individual plans choices and experiences that will enable him or her to learn lessons not covered in previous incarnations, or to repeat ones in which they have failed to learn the lesson. The objectives of the experience, the spiritual progression intended, will also differ depending on one's spiritual level, or as I prefer to say, spiritual age.

Conventional psychology and counselling cannot approach the depth of explanation that the spiritual perspective gives us. This is not a criticism, as until now, the spiritual insights have not been given to us. I felt an affinity with M Scott Peck, whose books have popularised the concept that the purpose of our suffering is spiritual growth. The point of it is to discover and then develop our spirituality. This seems harsh at first, but sense can ultimately be made from it, that would otherwise leave us adrift in a senseless vacuum.

As I am reminded by our guide, the soul has come to the body and the body to life, to progress its evolution by experiencing. What would you like for your life-lunch? Whenever we are faced with a decision that causes us to agonise over its making, when we are hit by slings and arrows and wonder why, this may well be fate knocking at the door, or in other words, life-plan in operation. We may then come to realise these events are not what they seem but spiritual tests we have chosen, challenges we have opted for to enable us to progress if we meet and overcome them. If we don't, then no big deal, we can take as many attempts as we like apparently, but we cannot "drop out"; we must experience every dish on the extensive menu of spiritual growth.

CHAPTER FIVE

SPIRITUAL LETTERS

As I related in the introduction, all information for spiritual teaching has come from our guide. I also said we have occasionally given spiritual letters to those troubled by the passing of a loved one. It is also refreshing for us to hear from another spirit, especially one with whom we had contact in the present life before their return to spirit. (Such contact is still through our guide, of course, as is all communication for those on Earth through their guide).

The first one of these letters I wish to reproduce is a letter from my present life brother to his wife. *"Why Come Back?"* detailed his tragic car accident. This left my sister-in-law traumatised. Five years after the event at the time of writing, she is still unfortunately wracked with anger and guilt at his passing. These emotions have caused her a series of health problems. My brother told me some time earlier in a similar personal message, that he and his wife were spiritual thirds. I knew this meant that, because of the spiritual connection, his widow would feel his loss all the more keenly. (Being thirds was unbeknown to both, of course, during their life together).

My earthly brother refers to the Three in his letter. Readers may have had messages of comfort from mediums with no reference to "Threes". It is only now that Spirit is allowing this knowledge to become available. All of these recipients had received mediumship sessions with us prior to the receipt of these letters and had received teachings about the spiritual truths, life-plans, the reason for the spiritual journey etc. This is why the letters carry such a degree of detail in this regard; to reinforce what had been previously channelled and to give perspective to it.

Roger J Burman

MY BROTHER'S LETTER

Hello Wink

I am really pleased that Roger and Angie are doing this for us. I have been trying to talk to you myself for so long now; I think you can hear me, but you put it down to your own imagination, you don't really know whether to believe it is me or not. When you go up to bed early and sit there with Brian and Arthur (their two pet cats), when they look into space, stare at nothing, it is me they are seeing. Especially Brian, my boy, he senses when I am there most of all. To be honest, I am there every night. You think about me so often, and I am drawn to you just as often. It is the place I want to be most though, near to you, so I don't mind.

I want you to know that when you visit the grave, it is only the place you put my earthly body. True that when you visit it, your thoughts bring me close to you, so I am there with you, but you can bring me just as close by thinking of me at home. I know visiting the grave is a sort of pilgrimage for you, but I know the depth of your love without the need for it. I know you feel some sort of satisfaction from it, and as long as it serves that purpose it is fine with me, but I want you to know I don't need you to do it, I know your inner feelings without it. So if ever you are unable to go, don't think you are letting me down in any way.

If ever you need to be reassured of my love in future, just read these words. You were my life, we were meant to be together, we were also meant to be separated early, a plan we made for our spiritual growth. What the separation has proved to us is that love can transcend death. Being physically apart does not diminish the depth of feeling, either on your side or on mine. I try to let you feel my love, try to let you know when I am holding you. When you wake in the night and say, "Is that you Eddie?" I am shouting yes, just let yourself believe that you hear me.

Adam, (their nephew) yes I do visit him. He thinks of me from time to time, usually when I have been to see him. He also speaks of me to you because he feels me around you, as I am so very much. He doesn't know that is the reason, he is not aware he feels me, as far as he knows I just "come to mind".

I am worried about your health, Wink. Your grief over me is the root cause of many of your health problems. Please realise, the last thing in the world that I would want is to be the cause of your illness. I know it is hard, but my dearest wish is for you to try and lift your spirits. I don't expect you to forget me, to think any less of me. Don't listen to those who nag you about getting your life together, finding a new man or a fresh start. If you want any of that, fine, it won't interfere with what we feel for each other, but don't think of it as a necessary thing to getting on with life. Getting on with life can mean just coming to accept our situation, accept that we love each other even though we can't be together, and be happy in that knowledge. Lift your spirits; look forward to each day because it is another day in which to celebrate our love for each other. Prove to all the rest of them the strength of our love. Prove it by showing the inner joy your knowledge of my love can bring, rather than by grief.

There is no guilt in having joy in your life. You are now living for the two of us. You know my feelings for you; I want you to know, too, that we will be together on your return to spirit and that we will share our experiences. Live for me, Wink, have joy and experiences in your life to share with me in the next. When it is time for you to return to spirit, your experiences will be an enrichment for us both. I need you to live for me as well as for yourself. I don't want you to be ill, I want you to be well, be happy, have happenings in your life, good happenings, that you can share with me when you talk to me in bed later. I am so close to you, that when you have joy, I have it too, even now, so it is for the two of us. You can talk to me about things that happen in your life now, knowing that I can hear you and will be eager to listen.

It is not your time for quite a while to come yet; you have plenty of time to have joy in your life to bring back to me. Don't blame me for leaving you, it was planned, it was meant to be. What we need now is for you to lift your spirits and live for the two of us so that the plan can be fulfilled.

Roger has spilled the beans now; we are thirds, Wink. Luisa, your guide is my guide too. Not as Luisa to me though, to me she was my sister Grace in England in the early 1800s in Wiltshire. Being thirds means that we have been together loads of times, you and me, you and Luisa with me as guide, or me and Luisa and you as guide. We will go on and on for thousands and thousands of years like this, so yes my love, I will be waiting for you and this is why I want you to live for us now. When you are enjoying life this is not a cause for guilt but for celebration because now you can think

"I can't wait to tell Eddie about this later tonight", knowing that I will be there, waiting and excited to hear about it.

I am going to leave it at this for now, Wink; this should confirm much of what you already believed and add a bit too. I love you, I always have. You are a part of me, one third of the whole that is us.

Eddie

I know there are many who long for contact with their departed loved one. Spirits try desperately sometimes to contact us here in this dimension. The film *"What Dreams May Come"*, while not completely correct in some of the ideas it portrays, does accurately show the spirit's frustration at trying to let the grieving ones know they are still around them.

In those that are spiritually sensitive, a feeling akin to cobwebs on the face is, I believe, quite a common experience denoting the presence of spirit. Practising meditation over a period of time will improve the ability to hear spirit, but I confess to laziness here. I have, however, stood on a ley-line and been able to see my brother in my mind's eye and hear him speak to me. Ley-lines enhance the ability for spiritual communication. I also felt his joy. We earthbound spirits need not fear our loved ones are not happy. (Ley-lines are a natural phenomenon, part of the Earth's energies. This is a large topic, which I will cover in my next book).

My next letter is from Angela's grandfather, Fred. He spent his life working on the land and had a natural affinity with it. He also spoke bluntly in life, as indeed he does in his letter, as you will see! His letter is revealing in a number of ways; he shows the soul can leave the body before death and shows a loved one can know our thoughts. He makes reference to Angela's former husband and many other personal aspects; Mill, of course, is Angela's grandmother.

Because of one past life as a Pagan, Fred has had restored to him on return to spirit, his knowledge of how to use the earth energies which he had in that incarnation. I use that part of his letter in my next book, but for now, here is his very personal message.

Why Come Back? Book 2

A LETTER FROM ANGELA'S GRANDFATHER, FRED

Well lass, this is the first time I have managed to talk to you, I have tried before but your chap here (our guide) would not let me for a while. He said you needed time to develop and move along your path a bit first; that the things I want to say to you would have more meaning when you reached a certain stage.

I knew you were with me, you know, knew that you stayed by me almost to the end. I wasn't in my old body for the last day and a half, I stood by the mirror on the wardrobe door and watched you all.

You were always my very good girl, right to the end you were that. You looked after Mill even though you were hurting inside yourself. I know that laddo gave you a hard time through it (Angela's husband). *I knew your thoughts when you came back that night. I heard you say "Thank God you're still here Grandad, I would never have forgiven the bastard if you had gone before I got here", but you would, you know, you don't have it in you to harbour a grudge, you are far too up the ladder for that.*

I saw the way you organised your Dad, don't expect more of him than he is capable of, my girl, you know he is a younger spirit than you and your mum were. He has grown in this life, I think you can see the difference in him from even fifteen years ago can't you, if you really think about it? He has a lot to learn, he is still a babe really in our terms.

I am pleased you found your other third; I know you are going to go from strength to strength, the two of you. I am pleased that you continue to care for Mill; I know she will miss you when you leave, but she is pleased for you really. I still look over her, you know, and I hear her talk to me when she is alone. She knows when I hear her, too, and will not be afraid to come and meet me when the time is right. I wasn't her other third, that was her Dad, but I know I am not due to leave until after she arrives, so we will see each other if she wants to. I do, she was a good old lass. I didn't make it easy for her sometimes, lots of times really. She nursed me when lots would have not. The mid-life upset was one of her choices, mental illness and its effects. (Angela's grandmother had a short period of mental health trouble occasioned by the menopause). *Both of us were changed by it, we both learned from it. Of course neither of us knew that then.*

As you know, I wasn't at all religious, only went to Church for Christenings, funerals and weddings, and not then if I could get away with it, but Mill used to want me to go, so I had to toe the line sometimes. I didn't want to go to your wedding, lass. I knew he was a wrong un, that he was going to be a bad match for you, but Mill said it wasn't up to us to make that decision and that you would be hurt if I didn't, so of course, I was there. I wasn't so far wrong though was I, lass. Me and Mill, we knew a lot more than you ever let on to. We saw what you didn't always realise we saw. We learned, spiritually we learned, from your experience, or at least I did when I got here, and I guess she will too, so it wasn't just you that needed it, we gained from it, too.

You and your new chap both have lots to do and I am proud to have been associated with you, lass. No, don't go and cry now, we've got this far, I can feel it welling up in you, what is there to cry about. I am in the place we all want to be, once we are here and remember. I had a good life, I worked with the land that I loved, I loved you and your boys, perhaps more that anyone really, and then Mill, we filled each other's life requirements and although it wasn't love of the romantic sort, we came to have a need and understanding of each other (love from a different angle again).

I love you lass, Grandad

My next spiritual letter tells another tragic story, the loss of a loved one suddenly, and at a young age and with no medical explanation. The couple were thirds again, which of course increased the feeling of loss the remaining one experienced. Here are extracts from a spiritual letter sent by the young man who is now in the spirit state to his remaining earthly third:

A LETTER FROM BRUCE

My dearest Kate

It is my one regret that I had to go in a way that caused such a shock to you, that I didn't have time to say goodbye properly. Once I realised I was dead, I came to you and was with you when you received the news. Your mother took a phone call telling her that I had gone. It was at a time when you were suffering physically yourself. It must have been really difficult for her to tell you and to cause you more pain. I really did not want to add to your trauma by giving you emotional pain to go along with the physical, but it was our time to part.

When I left that day, I knew as I was walking away that it was my time to go. I was so preoccupied that I even forgot to wave.

I know how often I am in your thoughts; if you try you can feel me when I am near to you. I look over you because I am your third. I saw when you visited my grave and thank you for the flowers, but want you to know that I am not there, that is only the shell that held the real me, we are spiritual beings having an earthly experience as I know Angie and Roger say. I am not there in that grave; you do not need to do this in order to be close to me. I am with you whenever you want me to be. You need only think of me to bring me close to you. You will hear me if you can open up to do so. Trust that what you receive in your mind is from me and not your own imagination.

I have shared many past lives with you as your third, hundreds in fact, and wish you to know that we will share many more both as partners and in many, many other relationships. You are spiritually more aware than you realise, and you can feel me if you trust that you can.

I have heard your question about the reason for my death and I can tell you that it was a rare, one in a million, defect that caused a failure of the part of the brain governing the respiratory system. The doctors missed it in examination and assumed it to be one of life's mysteries, much like cot death is in babies.

If you want to send messages to me, you can do it yourself, you know, you only have to think and I know your thoughts. If you are unsure about doing this, write to me, give it to Angie and she will gladly relay it to me for you. I must leave now, you know how I can talk, and we could be here all night. I send love, light and peace to you, and my heart is in your keeping until you return it to me.

Love, Bruce

My next letter contains quite a different message. It concerns an unhappy marriage and the husband's alcoholism. Peter, now back in spirit, can see his life from the spiritual perspective. He tries to explain this to his long-suffering first wife Linda. Peter is someone

I knew in this life, not as a friend or work colleague, but as a fellow professional, who lived and worked in the same town and whom I met for business reasons from time to time. I therefore knew of his liking for alcohol, but nothing of his family life. He does not mention his health problems in the letter, but I can add that he suffered with heart problems, dying well before normal retirement age.

PETER'S LETTER

Hello Linda. I wanted to communicate with you; wanted the chance to tell you things I could not have told you while I was alive; things that I did not know myself at the time.

I know I treated you and my children badly. I know that I failed you all and that I did not deserve any degree of love, loyalty or affection. I know I managed to effectively kill any chance of that in you all with time. I was tormented by it but unable to stop it. The drinking made matters worse, of course, but it was an addiction; I could not seem to stop it. No matter how many times I would promise myself that this was the last time, there was always another. I did not easily or openly admit that it was a problem, but I was aware of it really.

Through it and through my selfish use of my time, I missed the opportunity of learning the lessons being a parent can bring, I never really felt that I knew my children, but then I think they were probably better for me keeping my distance, perhaps that's one thing I did do for them without realising it. By not being close to them, my failure to support them emotionally, the family break up, the weakness that caused me to attempt suicide and my eventual demise was perhaps less painful for them than it might otherwise have been.

I never really meant the suicide attempts to be successful, you know, they were only the actions of a confused and floundering mind. I suppose I thought they would attract the appropriate attention, generate sympathy for me and in some way bring me help and support by making people aware that I needed it. The typical cry for help really. I know people blamed your leaving me for my first attempt. They didn't know the history of course, didn't know the real reasons why you left, why you were forced to look to another for what I was unable to provide. I could not bear the thought of everyone finding out how I had treated you, that I had systematically driven you away. I would have been blamed and that would never have done, so the suicide attempt was a way to make me appear the devastated husband and deflect the blame from me onto you.

From your point of view, the final insult I know was my failure to leave any provision in my will for our children. That of course, was only in keeping with the kind of man I had become, embittered and twisted. All my illnesses I now know were the physical manifestations of the confusion and sickness in my mind.

Now I am returned to spirit, everything is clear to me, and I wanted to share it with you. I cannot undo what is done, and it would not be correct to do so. We both chose that life together, hard as it is to believe, I know, chose to have those experiences, so although in an earthly sense I did wrong by you, spiritually I did right. I was supposed to be that way, supposed to have those dreadful experiences and provide them for others. It was a part of the spiritual journey to learn about love, to view it from all perspectives and to supply the experience for others to learn too.

On my return here, I reviewed as all do, what the life had taught me. I had the help of some others who I will call masters; I am not sufficiently high enough up the ladder to be able to see it all for myself, I needed their assistance. These masters helped me to review my life. I learned of the devastation the abuse and eventual dependency on a substance, be it alcohol, drugs or any other, can cause to the life of the abuser and to his or her family.

I saw how this could destroy love and care until it becomes anger and hatred. How any desire the family members may have to help the afflicted one eventually turns into blame of that one, or even a degree of guilt because of their inability to prevent the slide into addiction.

I learned about physical abuse, the need to hurt and lash out at those closest to you without any idea why, or any possibility of control.

I learned that through all of this, the love felt by the family members for the afflicted one is a long time dying. They cling to the belief that the afflicted one will improve, will return to the one they once loved, will win the fight against addiction. They will make plans and resolutions of their own conceived around the others addiction. When he is better we will..., if he would only admit his problem I will..., I wouldn't be thinking of leaving him if only he... and more like this. Against all odds they stay, far longer than can really be expected, to try and hold together the relationship, the family unit.

During all of this, for their trouble they receive more abuse, more hurt to add to the catalogue of hurt they already have. Others have little understanding of why people stay in this type of relationship, why they don't have what is seen as the self-esteem to leave it or the self-preservation to get out. This is the nature of love; once love has been felt for another it is a long time dying, even when active attempts are being made to kill it! You may think you no longer love this one who is causing you such pain when the truth is that if you did not love there would be no pain, or at least, not so much.

Think of the truth in this, if a stranger hurls abuse at you does it hurt or is it remembered for as long as abuse hurled by a loved one? No. When you cease to love you cease to hurt. The unfortunate fact is that once you have loved it is extremely difficult to stop. Even when a marriage is over, when each partner has found love elsewhere, the memory of the early love in that relationship, can still cause bitterness at its loss. The relationship may be over, the new one perfect in every way, but in a small corner of the heart will be this bitterness at the failure of the last one, only there because it is felt as a betrayal of the love once felt. It is the same for children who have felt love for a parent figure.

If one can learn to let go of that feeling, can forgive the partner that caused this hurt, can realise that to do so was in their life-plan, that it was there to teach about love from all angles, not just the moonlight and roses type, then they will be on the path to greater spiritual advancement. While this bitterness is carried in even the smallest corner of the heart, it will prevent true spiritual progression.

It is necessary to learn to allow that others are not always what you would wish them to be, to see that they have their own agenda, to love them faults and all, to take them as they are and not for what you hope they will become. When one can do this, a major spiritual lesson is achieved, a spiritual truth understood.

Realise that it was in my plan to be the way I was. On return here I understood immediately and realised that although on

Earth I was a failure at my relationships, in spirit terms, I had actually achieved the plan for my life, and assisted in the growth of you and our children in the process. You all learned lessons, painful ones it is true, but lessons that have taken you a step along the road to higher spiritual understanding.

They will not realise it until they return here themselves but believe me when I say that to carry the hurt now is to hurt yourselves, to hamper your own spiritual futures. I am told that you are higher up the spiritual ladder and that you have the capacity to learn to forgive, to let go the pain. If you can, you will reap the benefits, both in your current life and those to come. I say this not for my own sake but for yours.

On an earthly level I apologise, Linda, for what you endured, but on a spiritual level, I cannot apologise for having succeeded in my plan. As I now know you to be quite advanced spiritually, I hope you have enough vision to appreciate the truth of what is said here. You are now, I am told, with one who you have enjoyed happiness with before. The path is now to live this life in love and peace and not to allow pain and bitterness from what is past to get in the way of the future.

I send you my regards and my spiritual love and hope for your understanding.

Peter

To me this letter is such a "wow" from a teaching perspective, illustrating many points I described in *"Why Come Back?"* A so-called "bad marriage" is fertile ground for spiritual growth. It is hard for those that must suffer the experience, but as others have written, it is for the sufferer's highest good. This would not be a welcome comment I know, at the time!

As I wrote previously, the review of the life is as important as the life itself, which is amply illustrated in this letter. Thank you Peter and Linda for allowing me to publish it. On a personal note, Peter, I didn't think you were a bad sport, but of course, I knew nothing of your home life.

If the reader has not personally consulted a medium, they may not be aware what a testament to Angela's skill these letters make, as to hold the communication link and accurately type so much information is a rare quality. As I have not acknowledged her essential input to the writing of my books, I would like to do so now.

CHAPTER SIX

PAST LIFE MEDIUMSHIP

I now turn to our case files. Each person that has sought mediumship is different, in that the issues they are experiencing in this current life that have proved to have a past life explanation have varied. Even when the issues have been similar, the reasons for them having the issue have still been widely different. In many cases it is particularly noticeable that we have acted as a spiritual alarm clock. That is, we have advised the enquirer of a spiritual destiny. In some cases this has been a path they have already chosen and just wanted confirmation that they had made a correct decision. For others, it has been one they were considering because they felt they were not achieving their destiny, but were unsure what that was. As always, there is choice and they could ignore the call and return to sleep, or rise and shine (spiritually speaking).

In most cases, we see an enquirer once only. Some, however, return to us with further questions several or many times. This happened in particular with Eva and Cheryl and has allowed me to use a number of headings for both enquirers that usefully serve as pegs for information. These are:

- PAST LIFE CLUES – By this I mean, fears, phobias, reoccurring dreams, unusual sense of familiarity with certain people or places, particular aptitudes or skills and so on.
- HISTORICAL DETAILS OF INTEREST – This is information received about a past life that is not generally known, and of interest.
- LIFE LESSONS – Where it has been asked and the answer given, details of the spiritual reasoning behind an incarnation.

- ❖ TEACHING POINTS – If there is something of general application about the workings of spirit in a particular life.
- ❖ SPIRITUAL INSIGHTS – Any experiences that were unusual and not fully explicable as to their causes in the current life, but which point to spiritual contact and awareness.

EVA

My first person from the casebook, I refer to as Eva, a young mother at the moment, but an older spirit. Being such, she has had an eventful life to date. A big clue to her spiritual age was the details we were given about her guide, which is the first question we ask at mediumship sittings. The guide is an Egyptian from 3500BC.

PAST LIFE CLUES

As a six year old, Eva could read Egyptian hieroglyphics. Her teacher was amazed and discussed it with her mother. In her teenage years, Eva did some drawings that she now knows were Egyptian in origin. The answer to both these points is that she accessed a past life memory of her Egyptian life. As a child, both she and all around her were unaware this was a distant memory from another life, so it was not developed any further.

A second clue was Eva's intense dislike of having her head underwater. Her guide explained that this had a past life origin from a life in the early 1700s. In that life she was a fourteen year old boy, a slave being transported on a ship from Jamaica where he was born. The ship was *"Henrietta Marie"*. It sank off Key West. He was drowned in the sinking ship, being shut under deck with the other slaves.

The third clue is the most common one among older spirit, familiarity with important people in her current life. She asked her guide about her spouse. Her husband is not her spiritual third, but had previously been her father in two lives and her child in another; they had also shared an incarnation with him as tutor and she as student.

Eva has a friend from her schooldays with whom she shares a bond, but without understanding why. Upon enquiry, they had shared several lives together. They had been sisters, mother and son, and husband and wife. I could continue with this clue, but I think this is sufficient to show her as an example of an incarnation where many of the important people in life have a past life connection.

LIVES OF HISTORICAL INTEREST

I believe the ancient Egyptian life of 3500BC to be one such life. When spirit give dates BC, they are always approximate, we understand, due to the great time elapsed, and the difficulty spirit has with our time frames. In that life, the spirit that has remained behind in the current life as her guide, was an architect and she was his wife. She had two sons in that life, Asim, and Djet. They lived at Thebes and her husband was one of the architects responsible for the design of the temple of Isis.

She was of this planet but her husband was a visitor who came to bring to the planet the knowledge required to build the fantastic buildings that were familiar to his world. He was one of several visitors coming from a highly advanced world who formed the hierarchy of that time.

She was unaware of his real identity at the time of their life together. This is not strange, as the appearance of his race and ours was the same, or almost so. His race was an extremely spiritual one, and during their life together she developed spiritually. He taught her to read hieroglyphs. For a woman to read who was not of the Royal line was unusual, and it created some unrest in those about them. His occupation in the other world was that of architect and he brought, with others, the skills necessary to build the temples and pyramids that have continued to be a source of wonder in our world.

Before the first dynasty, Egypt was in fact two lands. The unifier of these lands was called Menes and known as the first mortal king of Egypt. Some date this as 3100BC, but it was in fact nearer to 3500BC. Menes was a traveller from her husband's planet. He founded the capital Memphis by damming the Nile to reclaim land for the city.

During this time papyrus was invented and as a consequence writing was used as an administrative tool of government. This created the conditions for prosperity, which can be seen in the magnificent artefacts that have been found from this period. The temple of Isis was relocated and a new structure built on a different site in later time and the temple of her guide's building fell in to disrepair. Today, information relating to this period is extremely hard to come by, and even if it is found, the accuracy should not be relied upon, given the great time elapsed, commented her guide.

Having started on a line of enquiry, Eva went on to ask why the pyramids were built as they were, and if there is more to them than is known. Her guide answered that the pyramids are not what they seem, and that the scholars of our planet are in no way near to the truth of it. Those nearer to the truth are usually labelled as of unsound mind! This information will not be generally known on our planet for quite some time to come, as it involves an area of physics that is not even discovered and will not be for many years.

The pyramids were not primarily burial chambers. Those of high rank were accorded the privilege of being buried in a pyramid, much as in our current time, those of high rank may be accorded the honour of being buried in, for instance, Westminster Abbey. It does not indicate that Westminster Abbey is a burial chamber because of this. This, in a very simplistic way, explains why our archaeologists have interpreted the pyramids to be burial chambers, the real reason being quite beyond their capabilities to discover at this time in our planet's evolution.

The pyramids were communication centres, used for communication with other worlds and also for spiritual communication by the highly evolved visitors. There is a dimension to them that is not accessible to us on Earth yet, as we do not have the knowledge necessary. The alignment of them is not by accident, and we were told, we should view the part seen as the visible part of the iceberg. As in the case of an iceberg, what is not seen is greater than what is.

LIFE LESSONS

Eva has a friend from schooldays, Karen, the feeling of familiarity with whom I previously referred to as a past life clue. They have, throughout their past lives, been sisters, mother and son, and husband and wife. They shared their last incarnation together in England, at the turn of the century during the reign of Queen Victoria. They were husband and wife during that life, Eva being the male and so the husband who lived and farmed in Kent. He suffered an accident with a threshing machine, which injured his legs and meant he couldn't work again. Karen his wife carried on with the farm and saved it for their children. At the same time, she nursed him and they shared a bond deepened by their care for each other.

In that life, the injury to Eva's legs provided the circumstances for a variety of lessons for the two of them. She experienced the lesson of a formerly independent and dependable person learning to rely and depend on others. She experienced the depth of love and care given by her then wife.

Karen on the other hand, experienced the opposite. Having relied on her strong and dependable husband to cure all ills and sort all problems, she found herself in the situation of having to take his role. Her first reaction was the purely human one in so many cases like this, of blaming her husband for having the accident and for failing her in this way. She came through this, however, to realise the spiritual truths sufficiently to become the close loving wife, his support and succour. That life was a success for the two of them, confirmed the guide.

TEACHING POINTS

In her current life, Eva has experienced during childhood, a severe problem relating to her hips, necessitating surgery when she became adult. One immediately thinks of her leg injuries as a farmer in the past life in Kent. Why is the leg problem repeated I wondered? The answer received was that if it so happens that a "prop" or circumstance is successful in achieving intended spiritual growth, it may be used again. This does not necessarily mean, therefore, that a second use of the same circumstance or "prop" is suggestive of a repeated incarnation following a failed one. It could in fact, indicate a circumstance that served well and assisted in achievement of the life lesson.

The reader may recall from *"Why Come Back?"* each one of us is a one-third part of a spiritual whole. We are together in the spiritual state, planning and reviewing each life. When spirit decides in their Threes, on the lessons to cover in a lifetime, they plan the circumstances that they hope will give rise to the opportunity for these lessons. When this current life was planned and the lessons to be learned were decided on, it was necessary to find circumstances that would give rise to the opportunities for them to succeed, advised our guide.

I have explained previously, that spirit thirds often choose to interact with spirits that they have "worked" with before, that collections of spirits come around again and again, particularly if they worked well together in a past life. In the same way, spirit may choose to use the same "prop" for their play as one that had a successful outcome before. The same basic ingredients served in a different way and with different players, can produce successful results again for the spirits concerned.

This is the way of it with Eva and leg problems. It worked well before, she was familiar with it and so it could be used again in order to produce some of the lessons of this life, both for her and others that she was to interact with. For example, looking after Eva impacted on her mother's life so one of the reasons for it occurring, was for her mother's spiritual growth. This counsel from her guide enabled Eva to understand that it was not a repeat of the leg problems because she was unsuccessful in her past life, but because she was!

A second teaching point also arises from Eva's current life. Her marriage was stretched almost to breaking point at times because she and her husband experienced one problem after another trying to buy a particular house. This was in the village in which Eva had grown up and was next door to her parents.

It was a kind of test for them; they both had inner feelings that this was the property they were meant to have, and despite all the problems they have retained it! That in its own way is a kind of proof that it is the place they were intended to be. I can personally confirm that whatever is important in a life-plan seems to be the hardest to come by. Things that happen easily are of less importance to the plan. This is the way of it, the harder it is, the more the value. Choosing what appears as the easier course may appear correct in earthly terms, but may not be so from the spiritual view.

SPIRITUAL INSIGHTS

I am sure everyone has them at some stage, to some degree: intuition, gut feelings, a sixth sense, spiritual divine grace and the particular meaning I use here, unusual experiences without a rational-scientific explanation. Eva had five such insights that we discussed with her and her guide, which I now describe.

1. In her early teens Eva stayed in a B & B on the Scottish borders and during the night had terrible stomach pains. She dismissed it as something eaten etc, but on the way back, stayed again in the same place and in the same attic room. She again experienced strong stomach pain, which disappeared when she left.

Her guide explained that there was a reason, but not a past life one. Eva was, at that stage during her teenage years, developing a spirituality that unfortunately became side tracked to a great extent until now. During this visit and in this attic room, she received the essence of a young girl who died there during childbirth. The girl in question had lived a traumatised life, suffering abuse at the hands of her uncle with whom she was obliged to live. Her pregnancy was as a result of the abuse, and she was confined to the attic room alone in order to keep quiet the situation. When complications occurred, she was without help and both she and the child died.

The girl in question was a young spirit, just starting out on life's journey, and because of the level of trauma in her life, was unwilling to leave and rejoin the others of her spirit Three following her death. She has since passed on to her correct place, and has worked through the trauma of that life. Eva, in that insightful stage and being a similar age to the girl, felt her presence without realising it.

2. When Eva was in Sri Lanka at a place called the Hill Club, she disliked it immensely. She had to go along a long corridor to the rooms and would have gladly run the length, due to the strange feeling she had about it.

Her guide confirmed again, that this was an indication of the level of awareness Eva can achieve. She had accessed a negative energy left over in the place from the death of a servant in the club. This was caused by being beaten by one of the members for failing to observe proper respect. The member was the worse for drink and went too far in the beating. Others restrained him, but not in time for the servant, who later died from his injury. The negativity left in that area is what Eva felt. Not a remaining spirit, just a negativity left in the ether caused by the violence.

Our guide added that this is one sort of thing that will require attention in due course, along with many others; the removing of negativity caused by man and his inhumanity to others, animals or the planet. This negative energy can have a damning effect on planetary health and any such affected areas will be in need of the attentions of those with the necessary expertise. (For more on this topic, please see my next book *"Who Will Heal Earth?"*.)

3. Eva was thinking of a girl she knows, who is Egyptian. She does not have an affinity with this person. While thinking of her, a bowl smashed, not in the room Eva was in, but in the one next to it. There was no real explanation as to why this might be. No one else was in the house; the bowl was safe on a wide shelf, in no apparent danger of slipping off. She asked her guide if there was a reason or if it was just coincidence.

Her guide answered by saying, *"Eva is correct and insightful in her dislike of this person. It would not be correct for me to elaborate on the reasoning for this, but I would ask that she is satisfied to know she has shown insight and that her instinct is completely correct in her dislike. I wished to send a sign to indicate that Eva was indeed having thoughts that were in accord with my own, and found this the only way to attract her attention, as she does not easily think of me, or that it might be me putting forward ideas to her."*

He then apologised for the destruction of the bowl, but said that it caused sufficient attention for Eva to remember the incident and seek confirmation, so it served well in this.

4. Without going into all of the detail, Eva believed that she had a premonition about a friend's death a couple of weeks before it happened and asked her guide to confirm if this was so. He replied

that he was attempting to prepare the way for it, and that she was correct in that assumption.

5. Eva had been wondering if she was being pushed towards working with children. She was finding things were happening almost too easily and sought confirmation that this was the way she was meant to go.

Her guide replied that Eva would have a special gift for working with children with disability of either a physical or mental nature. Children are the hope of the planet, they are the way forward, and many are returning with knowledge implanted within them for the tasks that lie ahead. As we had discussed with our own guide in other conversations together, children of a spiritual disposition need the gift nurturing so that it is not left to wither and die as they grow, allowing the materialistic nature of the world to take over. Eva was destined to have an affinity with children so that she would find herself able to be in the position to assist in this nurturing.

Her guide asked her to remember also, that the higher the spiritual level, the more difficult the life is that we choose for ourselves. This means that children with disability are often returning high-level spirit. They are special children, in need of specialist help. (Since this enquiry took place, I have become familiar with the books written about *"Indigo"* children, which are the same children referred to here.)

CHERYL

My next enquirer is almost worthy of a book in herself; we were delighted to find she had an intense curiosity about her past lives. The amount of detail she requested in the answers has resulted in our having volumes of notes from mediumship on which to draw and use for our own better understanding, as so many teaching points were illustrated in this way.

It was a sub-plot in her life to be paradoxically spiritually aware, yet at the same time sceptical, even of her own mediumship ability. This is something that most mediums experience at some time, but it was becoming a real handicap to her spiritual growth. She has, we have all observed, recently grown spiritually in leaps and bounds, so we feel this was a successful enterprise for all parties.

She is quite an old spirit; the first Earth incarnation for which we were given details, was 1246-1214BC when Cheryl was a Pagan living in Britain on the edge of the River Avon.

PAST LIFE CLUES

The enquirer, Cheryl, is quite comfortable with spiritual concepts. Indeed, she confirmed she had practised mediumship of the "evidence and comfort" kind in the past, although on the death of her dear friend and fellow medium Kevin, had ceased to do so. She lacked confidence to do this alone, having nearly always previously offered mediumship with this friend.

She had not attempted to obtain past life information for herself or anyone else, even though she has acceptance of past lives. She had once previously been given some details of a past life, including her meeting with a mercenary soldier called Miguel in the papal armies in 1503. This information had raised her initial interest in spirit. I have a total of fourteen questions that I have selected from Cheryl's mediumship sessions with us, that I categorise as past life clues.

1. Not surprisingly, the first clue concerned this past life information. Cheryl sought confirmation of the past life she had been previously given. Indeed, this was her guide, who appears to her as a Spanish mercenary soldier because that was the last shared incarnation together. (Her guide's words were of course transmitted through Angela's guide, as all mediumship is guide to guide.)

We confirmed this spirit is her other third, and looks after her as all guides do for their incarnated thirds. He is still with her, and will be so until she rejoins him. The other third was Kevin, and this is why she was so guided by his influence. Cheryl and Miguel have been together in other lives previous to that one, but not since, this is why he appears in that particular guise. He has reincarnated with Kevin again since then on occasions. Cheryl and Kevin have been together on four occasions in the time between her life with Miguel and the current life.

It is Cheryl's spiritual age that has made it necessary for her to come to spiritual awareness in this lifetime. It is quite fitting, or so we thought, that the event bringing her to the beginning of her awareness in the first place, was the giving of this particular past life information to her, which introduced her to Miguel, her guide and other one third.

2. Cheryl has a deep interest in the English King, Richard III, 1452-86. She has read many books of the period, collected pictures of him and is an active member of an historical society devoted to the era.

The reason for her being drawn to this era was easily explained by her guide: *"Cheryl was only a distant cousin to Richard III, but was greatly enamoured of the man. She saw him as the rising sun in her vision at the time. She was most struck by him and carried a regard for him her entire life."*

In this particular incarnation, she was Katherine Neville, a cousin on Richard's mother's side (Rabey). Her father was Edward, Richard's mother's brother. She had one son, William. The other name she was given in the mediumship session was Catherine Howard, which Angela thought was either mother or grandmother. Later she was able to confirm it was mother.

3. Cheryl had an aunt named Mary, for whom she had a fondness. Her affinity for Kevin has been explained. She next asked what past lives she had shared with each of them.

Her guide answered that Kevin had shared as her third, hundreds of lives with her, some before they incarnated here. He shared a life in North Norfolk that Angela had already given Cheryl some details of. He was actually her husband in that life. He was the one who incarnated with her in her life as Katherine Neville, but was a friend rather than relative that time.

Mary had shared four other lives with Cheryl, two of them in other worlds. In this world she was with her during the life she shared with Miguel, which is why they felt such a connection.

4. Her next question was intriguing. It concerned a childhood fear of bells being rung, and the dark. Her doctor had told her mother that this was something she would outgrow, but did not otherwise

have an explanation. This fear was with her in early childhood but did diminish as she grew older.

Her guide gave the spiritual explanation. He related that Cheryl and her family were executed in the 1300s, by burning. The sentence was carried out at sundown, and the bells were rung to summon the populace to witness this. This was a life in Spain and the reason for the execution was failure to agree to the wishes of the Spanish equivalent of a feudal lord. This personage was attracted by Cheryl who, as a wife and mother, rejected him. He accused her of witchcraft as an act of revenge, and so she and her issue were destroyed, as it was believed she would, as a witch, be in league with the devil.

5. Cheryl was in a hotel in Woodhall Spa, Lincolnshire. It is famous for having been used by pilot officers in World War Two. There were several bomber airfields nearby. Cheryl was standing in the hotel when she heard a voice say "Look behind you". She turned around, but there was no one there. There was, however, a photograph of Guy Gibson hanging on the wall behind her, the pilot of Dambusters fame.

She wished to ask if there was a reason why she has an attraction for Guy Gibson. Her guide replied that they had shared a previous incarnation and she has recognised him spiritually. To pre-empt the next question, he also advised that the incarnation shared, was as military companions in a different world.

6. Cheryl wished to ask if there was any reason why she was always afraid of her father till the day he died. Her guide suggested that if Cheryl were to investigate her feelings in this regard, were to analyse the fear, she would realise that it was not fear of the sort experienced when one thinks oneself in physical danger. Nor the sort of fear experienced by one used to regular physical abuse. It was a fear born out of her own wish not to feel that she had performed in a lesser way than his expectations of her. This was carried through from a life in which he was a strict and demanding tutor, and she his student. She had great respect for him in that life and suffered mortification if ever she did not fulfil his expectations of her. This carried through and became the feeling she thinks of as fear in this life.

She wished to know more of that life and her guide gave the following details: It was a life in Teotihuacan City in Mexico in which she was born in 104BC and died in 72BC. Her father in the life was a teacher of building skills and she was his student, a young man. The life was one of subjection to the will of another, of having one's life arranged according to their dictates. The young man that she then was, spent his life trying to live up to his father's expectations, something that given his unreasonable demands, was a near impossibility. The third in that life was Kevin who was a fellow student, they offered each other support through the time with the teacher.

7. In *"Why Come Back?"* I related how relatively minor purchases such as a book or a CD can be spirit inspired, by one's guide dropping in a thought. This point was nicely illustrated in Cheryl's next question. The first "adult" book she read at the age of thirteen was an Anya Seaton novel about Katherine Swynford, who is buried in Lincoln Cathedral; she had always retained an affection for it, rereading it often. Katherine Swynford lived from 1340 approximately to 1400. Cheryl wished to ask her guide if she had any connection with Katherine, as she had always felt an interest in the lady.

He answered by saying that the reason for this book coming into Cheryl's path was precisely to awaken her interest in history. She needed to have such an interest to further certain key points in her life-plan, and the book was very important in facilitating this. It was no accident that she read and developed a fondness for the book; because it has assisted her greatly in her plan and her inner spirit is aware of this, she has developed this affection for it. The person herself has not interacted with Cheryl in any way of spiritual importance, only the book, concluded her guide.

Cheryl raised a further point. She and her friend in this life would have been great great granddaughters of this lady (in the Katherine Neville incarnation), was this any connection she asked? The guide said that this is a fact that influenced it being that particular book chosen for the task of awakening Cheryl's interest in history, but no, he repeated, the interaction was with the book, not the person. Just a coincidence of sorts, although nothing is really coincidence!

8. Her next question was another one of those synchronicities! Cheryl had secured (against all her expectations) part-time employment at an historic building, a castle dating from the fourteenth century, now operated by the National Trust for England. She felt at home there, a surprise feeling for her given the nature of the place. She asked if she had any connection with the place in which she now works, from a previous life.

Her guide replied that yes, she lived there as a girl in service from the time the castle was first occupied. She died from a fever in the winter of her seventeenth year. Her elder sister was also in service there and that is who Cheryl often feels when she has a comfortable feeling. After this life, Cheryl reincarnated again quite quickly, within two years, which she found fits with another of her past lives.

9. Cheryl had a question that is frequently asked, concerning an affinity with animals, in her particular case, with horses. The answer received was not what one might first imagine it would be.

Her guide answered that in 1831-65, Cheryl was a male slave of a plantation owner in Jamaica. Her master called her James. She was a groom in the stables due to her affinity with horses. She possessed an almost uncanny knack with them. It was observed that it was almost as if she were able to communicate with them, which of course she could.

Her third in this life was Kevin who was female and her wife, named Martha by their owners. Martha lived 1835-65 and was a housemaid. There was a rebellion of the slaves in 1865 and both were killed in it.

10. Cheryl has an interest in herbs and the old religions, particularly the Pagan religion, Earth Mother and so on. She asked if she might know if there was a reason for this.

Her guide replied that in 1246-1214BC, Cheryl lived in Britain on the edge of the River Avon. She was a healer and a worker with herbs and she knew of and worked with the ancient earth energies, was in tune with them. She made medicine from herbs and knew the healing properties of many elements of Earth.

It is no surprise that she has an interest in ley-lines, herbs and earth matters in the current life. She was what we may now call a "white witch". She shared that life with Kevin, who was her father in the incarnation.

11. Cheryl has a friend of thirty years called Ken. He always calls Cheryl "Mother". "Is there any connection there please?" she asked.

Her guide replied that in 803-855 in Africa, Cheryl was Hasina, the daughter of Miguel, who was Nuru and lived 771-841. Ken was her son in this life, named Ekon. This was just a family life in a native village, nothing special really, just one of many such lives souls require to fill in gaps and cover repeat tasks.

12. Besides being Katherine Neville, Cheryl wished to know if she had any other Plantagenet connections, as she felt that she did.

She was correct confirmed her guide. Cheryl had an incarnation in which she worked as a lady's maid to Eleanor of Aquataine, who was later the mother of Richard I. Her name was Adorlee d'Allard and she lived from 1122 to 1183. This is why she later came back as a member of the Neville family because of her knowledge and connection with them.

13. Cheryl wished to know if she has been with a person called Jack Robinson in a previous life. He was one of the most influential people in her current life.

Her guide replied that she had a life in which she was born the daughter of a village priest and late in her life married her father's successor to the parish. Her name was Sarah Thorn. This was in North Norfolk, in the early 1700s (the Norfolk life briefly mentioned earlier). Jack was her father in that life. They were very close and he was a strong influence to her, nurturing her intelligence with more care than would normally been shown to a daughter in the era. As a vicar, he was interested greatly in theology. He was spiritually aware, but his occupation did not permit for the expounding of his inner beliefs.

Sarah Thorn was an unusual young woman. She took a great interest in theology, indeed had it been possible for females to join the clergy, she would undoubtedly have done so. She was encouraged in her interest by her father and later by her husband. She felt that there should be more to know than the usual teachings proffered by the church and investigated many "alternative" religions. This she did in secret due to the nature of the times, but again with her father's support and active participation. She was in tune with the earth energies, was clever in the use of herbs and healing energies. She was the one in the village that was always called upon when a woman went into labour, when anyone was ill or dying. She gave her time to the poor and needy of the village and treated many successfully with her medicines.

14. Cheryl likes the Holy Land, has a strong feeling for it, but does not believe the feeling to be connected to any religious belief on her part. In a reading she was given a life in the Holy Land, an ancient life. We asked if we could we have any information on this please?
   Her guide confirmed that she had an ancient life in the Holy Land, but only a short one. She was born in Jericho, the son of a tanner. At the age of 20 she contracted an illness from the water and did not recover. This was from 323 to 303BC approximately.

The many past life clues here prompt me to quote George Elliot, who I believe wrote once,

> "Our deeds still travel with us from afar
> And what we have been makes us what we are"

   Just as the details of my own past lives belie my current life appearance as a dull number cruncher, one who has a safe, steady occupation and knows of nothing much outside of that life, so with Cheryl. She lives a quiet, modest life in the countryside, and so one would hardly dream she had such a varied history to her make-up.
   She is younger spiritually than some of those in her present life-circle, and quite unnecessarily, appears at times to feel self-conscious and can be a touch sensitive about it. This is rather at odds with the usual human attitude of not liking to admit to advancing years!
   This only arises because here on Earth we are a comparing species; spiritual age signifies nothing other than one spirit has existed longer than another. There is no superiority or inferiority in one's spiritual age. To put this into context, a baby has not lived

as long as its grandparent and so will not have the same life experiences as the grandparent. It does not mean the baby is a lesser person, a less worthy individual, or that the grandparent is in any way superior, just that the baby has yet to complete its life experiences whereas its grandparent has already completed many.

A further analogy, which illustrates by contrast, is that of a twenty year old poor man and a forty year old rich man. When the young man has lived another twenty years, he may be forty, but he will not necessarily be rich! A level three spirit however, when becoming a level five spirit, will be equally enriched as all other level five spirits. It is all just a matter of time; some have been in existence longer than others. Skill and ability do not enter into it; we will all arrive at the final endpoint equal.

Spiritually then, we all arrive at the same destination; it's just a question of which station we have alighted upon to break the journey, just that some are further along the line than others, but we all start out and finish at the same point, the Collective. Of course, we don't just do it once. We may have been in previous Threes, of which we have no recollection, not even when returned to our natural spirit state.

LIVES OF HISTORICAL INTEREST

All periods have their interest, but the European conquest of South America is one that had far-reaching consequences. Columbus' voyage was celebrated in the film *"1492 Conquest of Paradise"*. That and the earlier film called *"The Mission"* portrayed some of *"the bloodlust and greed of government and even the church"* to quote from the cover jacket of the video.

The ancient civilisations of South America were destroyed and the future destinies of both Europe and the Americas greatly affected from this time onwards. Cheryl's life from this period is therefore the first one I highlight as having special historical interest:

1. Cheryl was Anna and was incarnated with her third, Miguel, who is now her guide, in the years 1503-08. She was a young French girl when they met. She had been orphaned and lived with an aunt and uncle. They were farmers in France, where it borders with Italy.

Cheryl believes the son she had in this incarnation, also called Miguel, went as a Conquistador to South America with Pesare. Her guide confirmed that this son was indeed a Conquistador and in South America, as she believed him to be. He followed in his father's footsteps, her guide was sorry to say, in his strength and brutality, which led him to a successful career on his chosen path.

Digressing a moment from the lives of Cheryl, we have interestingly had two other enquirers who have had past lives in this same period. One was a sailor, Francisco de Aeranda. He died at sea and his wife, suffering a melancholy state, never recovered and succumbed to a fever. He died on the 1492 voyage of Columbus.

The other enquirer had a spiritually most significant life in this era, which is pleasing to refer to as a sort of balance. He had an important life as a Spanish captain of one of the ships that took Conquistadors to South America in the first instance. In this life, he abhorred the sacking of the cities and the general treatment of the race by his fellow countrymen and took a stance by which he refused to take on board the spoils of the trip. He lost his commission and was imprisoned on his return to Spain as a consequence, but he had shown true humanity.

The other past life of Cheryl that we quote in some detail has a fascination from the human-interest angle. It would not be detail that got into the history books, as the reader can judge.

2. As mentioned, Cheryl was Katherine Neville, a cousin of Richard III. Her father Edward, Baron Abergaven, was the brother of Richard's mother, Cicely Neville. Her mother was his second wife Catherine Howard and they were married in about 1448.

Katherine married a husband who had no interest in her other than the connection to the powerful Neville family she could bring, and treated her poorly. She bore him a child in 1475 when she was aged 20 and died in childbirth. He was mortified, not by the death of his wife, but because he feared the loss of that which he had worked to achieve, were his connections to the Neville family severed.

The child, who Katherine's maid and companion had christened William, died too, shortly after birth. Her husband resolved to keep Katherine's death secret and so installed in her apartments, a girl he had been having a sexual encounter with. He had it made known that following the death of her child she was suffering from a sickness of the mind and so was able to keep her away from those who might notice that it was not in fact Katherine.

Later, the girl bore him a son who was named William too. When she died, much later in life, her death was recorded as that of Katherine.

The secret was kept by the few of the husband's family retainers who were actually privy to it. The only one who might have been a threat to him was her maid, who was Kevin incarnated as a female in that life. This maid had supported Katherine through the bad marriage and become a close confidante and friend in the process. He had her murdered following Katherine's death before she could alert anyone to the true facts.

The intrigue increases when I disclose that the husband from that life has reincarnated and played an unhappy part in Cheryl's current life. Who said bad pennies always return? We have assured her, however, that this will not necessarily continue to be so, and of course, even the most evil of persons, once returned to spirit, are beings of pure light and love.

LIFE LESSONS

I now would like to look at four experiences and give the related spiritual reasoning.

1. In her current life, Cheryl had a friend who committed suicide. She was deeply affected by his loss, more so than she would have expected to be given the connection. Could her guide explain please?

He answered that spiritually, there was a sub-plot for her in this life that involved this friend. It was not met before his death, as he took his freewill choice and returned before his time. He will need to return to complete major tasks left undone. Cheryl is not affected in her life-plan because it was only a minor sub-plot for her. Provided the rest goes well, missing it will not warrant a repeat. Her spirit however, was aware of the loss of opportunity to complete a part of its plan and so grieved more than Cheryl would otherwise have done.

2. The second lesson from the current life is, unfortunately, a more common occurrence than being affected personally by a suicide. It concerns the everyday "soap opera" scenario of a discordant family relationship. Cheryl wanted to know why she has a strange relationship with her son. She always seems to feel as if she is walking on eggshells with him. They experienced a rift, which has now healed, but it is at times an uneasy truce.

Her guide responded, *"As usual, the answer is that they chose this in their plans. Cheryl chose to have a traumatic relationship with one child. To experience the pain of loss of a child, even though the child was still on the Earth plane; to experience the reconciliation but to feel the underlying rift in their relationship. To be able to compare this with the depth of feeling and the relationship she has with the other child, and so more fully appreciate the other relationship in comparison.*

On return to spirit, she will see this from a spiritual perspective. See the benefit she has gained in fully understanding the nature of mother love from the experience.

It is not written in the plan for this lifetime to overcome this situation. It is quite acceptable for it to continue as it is. If it were to be overcome, then an even greater lesson would be learned on return to spirit, but this would take a leap of progression on both parts. One cannot do it alone and it is not really in her son's plan to achieve such a leap this time.

For his part, he chose as part of his plan to experience this trauma in his relationship with his mother; a distance from her that he will feel and seek to compensate for during his life. He is fond of his mother, but still feels the need to 'joust' with her. He feels that his relationship is not the same as others have, and because of this searches for the missing element. He wishes to improve his situation but seems unable to prevent himself from antagonising it instead. This is all in his plan and will serve him on return to spirit; to see the nature of a mother/child relationship as it should be, by comparison to what it should not.

For this reason, he chose Cheryl as his mother so that their plans could complement each other. Again, on return to spirit he will assimilate that information together with other information gained in other incarnations, and learn from it.

A further part of his plan is the search, in his relationship with a partner, for the relationship he feels he should be able to achieve with his mother and may well explain the reason he seeks partners older than himself."

That was certainly not a standard "soap opera" response to a question! As I noted earlier, some of our mediumship turns into spiritual psychotherapy for the enquirer, and this is an excellent illustration. This is quite an alternative explanation to conventional theories. One day perhaps, life-plan will be the first thought, rather than the last.

3. The third lesson involves the life with her guide in the years 1503-08. Our guide gave us the following enlightenment to give to Cheryl, passed to us through the good graces of her own guide:

"Miguel was a character of strength and brutality to those around him. He had not experienced love in his life, the feeling of tenderness was an alien feeling to him, and he did not understand anything of gentleness, tenderness or love at all. That is until he met Anna. This young girl awoke in him feelings that he did not understand, feelings that were completely new to him.

First, he wanted to protect her. Now this was a real shock to his system. That he should seek to protect someone out of desire, out of his care for them, rather than for monetary reward, was in itself unusual. It was important to him that she be shielded from the knowing of his past brutality and the horrors and atrocities that he had committed, in fact, it was of paramount importance to him. She became the centre of his universe; from him she knew only tenderness and love, although she did have this feeling that he was himself surprised to discover this side of his nature.

She died in childbirth and he was devastated. He renewed his activities with a burning anger inside him, anger that this one thing of goodness in his life had been taken from him. This created an even more brutal edge to him and he developed a cavalier attitude to his own safety along with this, which made him a formidable force. It was this cavalier attitude that led to his demise and Cheryl was correct in her belief of the means of that.

Her lessons from this life were first, to witness the care and regard of this giant of a man; his gentleness with her and his interest in her welfare; to see how love can change the very core nature of a person. She also had the care of her nurse and the close connection there. (Her nurse was Mary, an aunt in this current life). *She would have followed this man to the end of the Earth in her devotion. Her life was short but memorable, her lesson learned, a true lesson of love."*

In human terms we think of longevity as a wished-for goal, an achievement, and think of early death as somewhat tragic. In spiritual terms, of course, longevity itself is of little value, only the experiences worked through compared with the plan. As we shall see in chapter eight, some lives can be planned to be very brief indeed. All plans have the exploration of "unconditional love" as their core and this life amply demonstrates it, in what at first sight, were apparently unlikely circumstances.

4. In the past life clues, we referred to a life 1122-83 when Cheryl was Adorlee d'Allard. Her guide in this life was her incarnated one third in that one, Raoul De St Denney from Province, a Master at Arms to King Louis. Cheryl believed she went with Eleanor of Aquataine to France, but did not go on crusade or to England but remained behind to look after the baby; Raoul also remained behind as captain of the guard or something of the sort.

Her guide confirmed this and added that her knowledge of history is an advantage, not the problem she seems to think it is. Having a good knowledge of the era should make it easy for her to visualise the information she is receiving and so appreciate it even more. Of course, she will have a keen interest in this period; it covered important incarnations for her.

She further asked what the lesson for that life was. Her guide responded, *"Yes, this was a genteel life, quite different to the one Miguel experienced as Miguel! The lesson was learned through the fact that Adorlee's husband worshipped his young wife. He quite simply adored her, so much so, that he set aside his own feelings of inferiority and jealousy to allow her liaison with Raoul that made her happy and gave her the children she so desired. Adorlee was aware of his generosity and came to realise the depths of a love that can put the needs of the loved one before one's own to such an extent. She developed a love for her older husband, not the kind of passionate love for Raoul, but one of kinship and gratitude. This illustrated the difference yet again of love in its many forms".*

TEACHING POINTS

1. One of the past life clues revolved around having once been a servant in a castle where Cheryl is now a part-time employee some six hundred years or so later! She shared that incarnation, as mentioned, with a sister. Cheryl wished to know, since she was able to feel the spirit of her sister in the castle from that earlier life, why she was still there.

Her guide answered that she is not. She draws close when Cheryl is there. She is a lower level spirit and still requires earthly guise and familiarity in order to feel comfortable. She has had some incarnations since that life, but that was a major one for her. She likes to revisit but can only do so when Cheryl is there to create the bridge.

This is one explanation for ghosts of an historical appearance; they appear in the form of the last shared lifetime, a fact possibly not known to the one experiencing the visitor! I discuss some of our own ghost encounters in the next chapter.

2. A second teaching point is the entirely logical assumption, but misconception, that having spiritual awareness is an indication of an older spirit. Cheryl has a son who she feels, has spiritual tendencies. "Does this mean that he is an older spirit please?" she asked her guide.

Her guide replied, *"I can tell you that he is not a complete beginner. Remember though that it is not necessary to be high-level spirit to display some spiritual awareness, lower level spirits can also have some degree of spiritual awareness in a particular life. It may not show itself in future lives, it may just be a flash of insight in one."*

I discuss in the next chapter this point in more detail, in the context of spirit levels and mediumship. What can be even more confusing, is someone who publicly states they are of a high spiritual level, and may genuinely believe themselves to be so, may in fact not be. To human eyes, there is no hallmarking or its equivalent for spiritual age, but what is usually indicative of age is the quality and precision of the communication and the accurate relevance to an enquirer. I visited several mediums in the period of my own quest for life's meaning and did notice quite a variation in communication abilities.

3. The third teaching point would be of almost universal interest. In our modern culture, it is easy to find oneself money rich, but time poor; to feel stressed, unfulfilled and possibly suffering from health problems that are lifestyle related. What is the secret of obtaining inner peace? Cheryl had felt inner peace for periods, but she seemed unable to keep it.

Our guide answered her question: *"When Cheryl starts on the path of fulfilling the destiny of this life, she will have little problem retaining the feeling of inner peace. Her life will be one of peace as she works. No one really has true inner peace until they find their destiny and set the first foot on the road to achieving it; they may think they do, but they don't really know it. Once you start, as both you and our brother* (i.e. Angie and Roger) *can confirm, the inner peace is with you for most of the time. The further you go along the road of your destiny, the greater the feeling. It would not be conducive to achieving your life-plan if you were to find inner peace before you found your destiny, you may settle comfortably with that and fail to proceed further."*

So there it is! The secret is my adage of "Find and Fulfil Your Destiny". In Cheryl's case, we may reveal that her destiny is working in a spiritual way for the benefit of others. Doing something other than for self-interest forms an important part of the multifaceted nature of love. There is much more that could be written (and has been) on this topic, but for now, I wish to conclude the account of Cheryl's mediumship sessions with a final teaching point and a discussion around it.

4. The final teaching point may hopefully give some comfort to those who have experienced a stillbirth. Cheryl's first baby was stillborn. She has now discovered that the same soul often reincarnates to the same mother. Her guide reconfirmed this can happen and frequently does so, perhaps more often than not, but in this particular case it is not so.

We are aware from the questions of another enquirer who had a stillborn sister, of one possible spiritual explanation for stillbirths. It was her sister's plan at the time to "experience" what is ingested by the foetus whilst in the womb. It is not fully realised yet, although recently research is beginning to get the ideas, just how much of the mother's emotion, nature and own experiences are experienced by the foetus. In reality they experience a great deal from the mother.

The plan for this other enquirer's sister, was to feel the animosity of her mother towards her unborn child, to experience the confusion of emotion from the mother and the fear and helplessness that manifested in anger. Having experienced this she has no need of a physical life and could return to spirit quite easily. Her contact with her spirit third on Earth was with the nurse who delivered her, a stillborn child. She felt the emotion of the nurse even before she left the womb. The birth had a profound effect on the nurse in question and shaped her destiny so enabling her to continue on her path. In this case it was not exactly that she chose not to incarnate, more that her plan did not require her to. She had completed it whilst in the womb and in this instance, at the moment of conception incarnation was complete, so in a sense, she did incarnate.

We also had an enquirer whose mother had a miscarriage in the early stages of pregnancy. Her guide confirmed that this was intended, for the spiritual progression of her mother.

This is a useful point at which to consider the debate over the ethical issue of abortion. The debate fails to recognise that abortion is either in the life-plan, and so an intended event, or a "wrong choice" and the soul will reincarnate at a future opportunity. Our guide advised that when abortion takes place, it is usually for the spiritual evolution of the mother or another with a close biological relationship to the foetus. Occasionally a soul wishes to have the experience of knowing that it was unwanted and so disposed of by its biological mother. Another lesson in the complexity of love for both parties.

In many cases, the soul will not yet be present by the time of the abortion and if this is a wrong choice for the mother, then the soul who was expecting to occupy that vessel will need to find another. If it was in her plan, it would be known that the foetus was not to be born and so a soul would not have chosen it unless it wished to. On the occasions when a soul has entered the foetus and the mother makes a wrong choice, then there may well be a repeat for both parties involved.

There is a point to clarify here about full consciousness, to reconcile what appear to be conflicting statements, firstly, that at the moment of conception, incarnation is complete and one's spirit guide is with one from that moment on, and secondly the statement that the soul will not be present by the time of the abortion.

The soul does indeed incarnate at the moment of conception. This is fact; immediately conception has taken place, the soul has "joined" with the foetus, which will be its vessel for its incarnation. I have related that nothing can live without a soul, no soul, no life. So, the soul has "joined" with its intended vessel to enable life to occur.

Depending on the need of the spirit concerned, the point at which consciousness enters the foetus is the element that can vary. The spirit that joins with the foetus may wish to experience:

- ❖ The mother's struggle and emotion as she undergoes the mental decision to abort the pregnancy.
- ❖ The animosity she may have towards the foetus for her predicament.
- ❖ The love she feels for it, if she is forced to abort on medical grounds or for social reasons.

In any of these or similar scenarios, the sprit will join with the foetus in full consciousness early in the pregnancy to take full advantage of this. If there is to be an abortion, and the only thing the spirit needs to experience is the abortion itself, then it may only come to full consciousness shortly before it. If the spirit only wishes to observe the effect its termination has on its mother, then it may not need to enter in full consciousness at all. The difference in pregnancy is not when the spirit joins the foetus, this is always immediately, but when full consciousness enters the foetus. This is the variable.

"When is the last time that a foetus may not have the full consciousness?" I asked. Our guide responded that full consciousness will always enter a foetus by the end of the fifth month, more usually much, much sooner. This is often the explanation for babies that do not appear to move much in the early months.

I asked our guide if all human pregnancies are intended events, and that presumably the fertilised egg will not go on to grow without a spirit present? Our guide confirmed that the fertilised egg will not go to full term of the pregnancy and eventual birth without a spirit present, but it is also true that all those with a spirit present do not necessarily go to full term and birth.

There are occasions when all a spirit requires are the experiences to be gained in the womb. It is true that all pregnancies are intended events, even if the intention is that the baby is unwanted, aborted or miscarried.

I would like to thank Cheryl for agreeing to share so much information about herself. She has amply illustrated past life clues and given us a number of life lessons and teachings to enlighten everyone, besides entertaining us with some of her past lives. Cheryl shows what a treasure chest of information about ourselves can be unearthed through mediumship. Enlightenment is seeing ourselves not as the age of our body, but far older; is realising our psyche is far more deeply rooted than just our experiences since birth; is realising the purpose of life is the accumulation of experienced aspects of love.

Although we have met a number of spirits who consulted us for mediumship, I wish to limit my writings to Eva and Cheryl, as there are other topics I wish to include in this book. Chapter eight returns to the mediumship casebook, but in that chapter, I concentrate on specific points and do not discuss in depth any one person. Before that, I wish to look at the topic of spiritual contact.

CHAPTER SEVEN

WE HAVE CONTACT!

This chapter is devoted to a discussion of contact with spirit in its various forms, starting with ghosts and ending with more description about the spirit guide. In between I discuss the following questions: Does having spiritual ability mean the person is an older spirit? How does one recognise spiritual contact? Do crystals help? How do alternative therapists work with spirit? Are one's dreams one's own? How does one stop an energy drain in the day? Is there any truth to the existence of fairies? Can one heal oneself?

GHOSTS WE HAVE MET

Readers of *"Why Come Back?"* may recall the discussion in chapter nine, of ghosts with an historical appearance and the several reasons confirmed why this phenomenon might occur. Angela and I have had several ghost encounters. In two of these, the spirit concerned has stayed around a building important to them; home in the case of one and employer's residence for the other. This is because they had happy memories from their life associated with the house and did not wish to move on. In contrast, one young man had a most tragic story, which I now relate.

He remained in what is now a public house but which was a private house when he lived there. The current owners are unaware of him, as he does not attempt to make his presence known. We encountered him one evening having called in for a drink and Angela asked him what he was doing there. He said he had sided with the Royalists during the English Civil War, against the wishes of his mother, who forbade him to fight. He had left home and secretly enlisted. He was wounded in a battle and came back home where he died. He was waiting to meet his mother, wishing to ask her forgiveness for the pain and suffering he realised he had caused her by his actions.

Angela explained she was not there, that she would have rejoined spirit long ago. He could not understand this; he felt sure that if she were in spirit, she would wish to see him because of the great love they bore each other in the incarnated state. Angela explained that he might not necessarily meet his mother in spirit, no matter how great their earthly love, unless she was his third. From the conversation, it transpired that he was in contact with the spirit world but could not find his mother there, so was waiting for her in the earthly location he had last shared with her. It also became clear that his mother had perhaps been an older spirit, and Angela explained that younger spirits cannot choose to see older ones, unless the older spirits wish to visit them. If this were not the reason he could not find his mother, then it may be because she had already incarnated again!

This would be the most likely case as he had been waiting for three hundred and fifty years, "a really long time", she told him. "Is it?" he responded. It did not seem to be so to him. Obviously his much loved mother was not his third, so she asked him about his third, what was this important part of himself doing while he waited around for his mother? He said that he needed to check with "his master" that he could discuss his third, as on Earth he believed, it was not known about thirds. He returned, and among other things, confirmed that his third was still waiting for him in order to have the life review. He realised now that there was no point in continuing to wait for his mother; that he should return and allow his thirds to review the life and he appeared to be happy to move on.

Angela enquired of our guide, how it could be that if the spirit of the young man was in contact with the spirit dimension, knew of his third and asked permission of an older spirit to speak of it, then how was it he did not realise that his mother might have incarnated again, or that she might be an older spirit with a different agenda.

He replied that spirits might be required to undergo certain things in their spirit state as well as in the incarnated state, in order to experience what is known. He had already told us that all is known in spirit; every spirit, from the moment of splitting from the Collective, has access to all knowledge; what they require is experience of the knowledge. We were aware that every incarnation is for the express purpose of completing a syllabus of experiences to learn about unconditional love. What we did not realise until that moment was that some of the experiences also take place in the spirit state, as an addendum to an incarnation.

Although the young man was in contact with his spirit thirds and his spirit mentor whom he called master, it then became obvious to us that they were allowing him sufficient time to reach the discovery by his own means, for his spiritual growth. Angela was concerned that she had then spoken out of turn; had supplied information that he was supposed to work out for himself. Our guide answered that no, it was correct for her to speak so. In this case, we were the pawns in the game who arrived on cue to supply a missing piece of his jigsaw puzzle so that he could move on to the next step in his journey.

This encounter took place in a crowded bar on a Saturday evening, with people anxious to eat, drink and smoke their fill. Everyone except us was unaware of the historic ghost in their midst, a young man with remorse, wishing to ask his mother's forgiveness for disobeying her wishes; a young man who regarded three hundred and fifty years as not long at all! This was a most unexpected "encounter" with our order for two gin and tonics.

The second encounter was a spirit resident in a very old cottage, recently bought and renovated by a friend. This friend became aware of her "visitor", when her electric blanket regularly appeared to switch itself on if she forgot on a cold night. Her husband on several occasions heard piano music, but was unable to find the source. Finally, when playing the piano or listening to piano music on CD, they both became aware of a "feeling" in the place. It did not worry them, however, as it was a nice feeling, peaceful and happy. The friend thought the visitor was upstairs rather than down, so Angela went in search. She made the acquaintance of the lady, who had lived in the cottage some two hundred years earlier. Being a young spirit and in no hurry to move onwards, she had not reincarnated, but regularly visited the area. Now that the cottage was once again a happy home with children, she had chosen to revisit it. She particularly loved piano, and this had drawn her to become more "noticeable".

Why Come Back? Book 2

Another ghostly resident was encountered in a hotel in which we stayed. The hotel is one used regularly for business seminars, weddings and other functions. The spirit had been the housekeeper there when the building was a private home in Victorian times. She remembered a pain in her chest, while making a bed. We assumed from this, she had suffered a sudden heart attack and died. She seemed to be a young spirit, a little confused about the need to hurry back to the spirit state. She commented on the fact that she liked to be around the people that now visited. She said the family had house parties in her day, but nowhere near the size of some of the ones now! We then realised she was not fully aware that it was now a hotel, as she believed the people were houseguests!

Just to show we are not alone in these experiences, I relate a question put to us by an enquirer, Peggy. She detected a spirit presence in her house, which is drawn to her son. It has been with the house all the time, but seems brought out by her son. She asked Angela about this in a mediumship sitting.

Her guide explained that the spirit attached to the house was called Mary McAindris; she had lived on that site in the early 1600s. She lost her son to a plague when he was aged fourteen years. This was her only child, as due to the complication of his birth, she was unable to have more. She has not moved on to return to spirit, being unwilling to leave the place where she feels his love and memory. This is unfortunate, as were she to do so, her spirit would no longer require the retention of the memory in the same way. She was drawn to Peggy's son at an age similar to that of her own son when he died, and has remained drawn to him from this time. If she is encouraged, she may well return to her spirit state, concluded her guide.

Another encounter was a most unusual one. It concerned a spirit that planned, before incarnation, to remain at a certain location following physical death. The reason for this was that the spirit had planned to come to the knowledge of the earth energies whilst incarnated. During her life, she lived close to an important site, that of Bloxholme in Lincolnshire, England. She knew of its ancient use, but was alone in her knowledge at that time, and the time was not then correct for her to use her knowledge.

She had died some eighty years previous to our encounter, having waited patiently for those who were to follow her; waited to see that they would identify enough of her clues and find enough information to continue with the work of the site. Once satisfied, she could go in peace, knowing the work would be in good hands and the task would come to fruition. I am pleased to add that in October 2001, the group now at Bloxholme reconstructed and reactivated the stone circle that had stood there in ancient times. The guardian spirit was then happy to leave and rejoin her Three, her task at last completed.

SPIRIT LEVELS AND MEDIUMSHIP

There are many excellent platform mediums and a growing number of other skilful mediums publishing messages for which they have been the conduits. I asked if this means all such mediums are older spirits?

Our guide replied saying that the mediums, even those who write the books and give messages may be older spirit, but are just as likely to be young or middle aged spirit. By finding the ability to connect with spirit, they will possibly have succeeded in their major plot for that lifetime. It does not follow that they will retain the ability into another life, however, but many discover it all over again when reaching level five. For clarification, this does not mean that all level five spirit has mediumship or other spiritual ability either, but it is quite common at that degree of development.

I have written previously that Earth is composed mainly of young spirits with some older spirits and a small amount of those in between – some of these may be the more successful 'basic message' mediums without being older spirit philosophers. I apologise if this hurts the feelings of anyone, this is most definitely not the intent! I have noticed human weakness and foibles in some who have the trappings of advanced spiritual communication and this is what prompted the enquiry.

I noticed feelings of self-importance in some; no doubt encouraged by having abilities possessed by only a few, and so feeling, maybe even unconsciously, superior. For instance, I have met a past president of a large spiritualist church, who clearly was most conscious of his past office and jealous of anyone who may appear more gifted or appear to have more knowledge than he had. He was not the open-minded, highly curious person I would have expected from one who had held such a position. An impression of closed mindedness mixed with spiritual abilities, is a clue to me of a young gifted spirit rather than an old gifted one.

I do not wish to make any sort of generalisation here. Many with spiritual abilities are indeed, gentle, caring, unassuming people, wanting nothing more than to use their gift for the good of others; willing to share all of their knowledge gladly and assist others in their spiritual development. It is my belief that this is true spirituality.

A similar point arises here about the specific ability to give spiritual healing. The person may be of any spiritual age; spirits at all different levels of progression are able to work in this way, but older spirit is usually identifiable by the high quality of either the healing or mediumship. Healing given by a spirit may be useful in both the spiritual growth of the healer, and as a means of enhancing the growth of others, as well as the benefit of the actual healing. Lessons may also be learned through the granting of the ability, both positive and negative lessons, our guide advised.

I have heard spiritually aware people speak in awe of someone as being "a master", whom they have met or read about. I am personally wary of anyone who describes themselves in such a way. Our guide advises that a spiritual master may not know that he or she was a master during the incarnation; those that do know while incarnated that they are masters, would certainly keep such information to themselves and seek to influence others by example only, not by claiming superiority.

We have only met one master ourselves. At least, we met a young person who radiated such a high level of energy, I can only attribute it to the fact that she is a master. She herself has no suspicion of her spiritual level, only that she knew herself to be particularly sensitive to the energies of persons around her. She becomes extremely emotional whenever she is in the company of any other spiritual person, and is acutely aware of changes in spiritual vibration. She has a destiny which spirit was not prepared to disclose fully to us, as they judged the time not correct, so it is a case of "watch this space" as her destiny unfolds.

DIFFERING CONTACT WITH SPIRIT

This can be in many forms and denial can have adverse health consequences! Seeing flashing lights in a room is one possible early form of spiritual contact. It is not intended to be any more than that, a beginning of contact. Some enquirers have been alarmed at the experience, but they can be assured that there is no harm occasioned or evil portent. It is just spirit saying "hello", a way of showing presence.

Of course, the most common form of contact is the indirect one of synchronicity. We are often unaware of the phenomenon, putting it down to coincidence when we do have recognition of it.

An example of synchronicity one enquirer experienced over a single weekend was rather unusual in its frequency. She has a serious health problem and had been told that radiotherapy was the prescription. She was aware from her own researches that diet could help her. She went shopping to a neighbouring town and met a complete stranger over a cup of tea who had experienced the same amount of radiotherapy she had been recommended to undergo. She learned much from the meeting.

She was in another shop and overheard a conversation the manager was having about food sensitivity, the very thing she herself had been exploring. She booked herself on the next available course. There was a particular health food supplement she was looking for and which had proved to be unavailable in her hometown, but this same shop had a supply!

She had been told part of her problem was with the flow of her energies, and this was contributing to her ill health. She had been recommended on the Friday of that weekend to consider Tai Chi, and at a car boot sale on the Sunday, just two days later, found a video for Tai Chi on sale! She had also been recommended to try acupuncture and that same day found an acupuncturist on the internet who lived nearby but of whom she had previously been unaware. The weekend newspaper she read carried an article about alternative therapy for under-active thyroid, and the previous day she had been recommended by her medical practitioner to double her thyroxin medication! When the guide gets going, he gets going!

That enquirer was sufficiently accepting of spirit to be able to recognise the invisible hand of her guide. In contrast, even where contact is less subtle than synchronicity, recognition can sometimes fail. One enquirer complained of hearing voices and difficulty in sleeping as a result. Upon enquiry, this turned out to be the female spirit of a stillborn sibling who is frequently with him. As readers may know themselves, it is true spirit that can be felt and this enquirer does feel it. The candles do gutter when she arrives, but this again can be a natural phenomenon and is no indication of anything sinister. His guide confirmed that the spirit visiting him has only good intentions; he should not feel intimidated by the presence at all, but open to it.

The guide went on to say that this spirit is not his third, but has a close connection to him due to their previous shared incarnations. He has an extremely spiritual nature and could if he chose, work extremely effectively spiritually. As we know, this must be a freewill choice, but that does not stop spirit trying to give a subtle push in the right direction!

In this instance, the enquirer's own guide has enlisted the help of others in his close spiritual group in order to attempt to steer him on the right path. If he does not wish to work in this way, he can say so and ask for the contact to stop. If he is sincere in his wish for this to happen, really wants it to stop, then it will do so. It is his guide's belief that he does not wish for it to stop however! If he once opened to spirit and started working in the way his guide knows he is capable of, he would no longer lose sleep.

Losing sleep, suffering headaches, all these can be side effects of blocking advanced spiritual contact, as Angela knows from personal experience! She remembers when she tried to deny her guide for five years! He says that he knew this was not her true wish but a manifestation from her earthly trauma and so he did not leave her, hence the many headaches she suffered!

I have detailed instances of spirit contacting us. What about the other way around? My next case history concerns a spiritually aware person who had made a pact with a like-minded friend that upon the death of either, the one in spirit would give a conclusive message to the one remaining. The point to be made is a spirit will communicate only when it is ready to do so. One of the friends died and the other duly consulted a medium. There was a message, but it was an unemotional experience and quite unlike the fulsome, detailed contact she was expecting.

Some years later through Angela, the spirit concerned related that in the early sitting, he was just fulfilling his half of the deal, nothing more, as he was not then ready to communicate. He also said that when returned to spirit, the soul assumes its true spiritual nature, remembers its true spiritual emotions and unconditional love. It loses the earthly aspects of its past life nature and uses them only to identify itself to one with whom it wishes to communicate. It no longer has a use for them in the spirit realm.

This enquirer had, through Angela, precise and emotional contact with her friend in spirit. He chose his moment, which was not until quite some time after his demise, when the message he gave had much relevance to the life-plan of the one remaining on Earth. (In this instance, the two were spiritual thirds, which helps explain his last remark, as all spirit thirds have a vested interest in the success of the lives of their incarnated counterparts).

Spiritual contact is not limited to one's guide or to those spirits who take a close interest in our lives. Let us not forget we may have spiritual contact with our beloved animal friends. There is an interesting point to relate concerning an enquirer and her pet pony. This lady and her pony had a really strong bond. For the whole of the time she was in labour the pony walked up and down along the fence and stopped immediately the baby was born at 2.10pm.

The connection with the lady and this pony was not a past life one. She has long had within her the stirrings of an ability to connect to nature, waiting for the time when it was to be used. This particular horse had a mind connection with her and this was enhanced because of her abilities. During her pregnancy, as often happens, this ability was even stronger that usual. It was this that caused the behaviour of the horse. Her guide went on to advise that she need not worry because she is unaware of how to harness the ability, this knowledge will come to her when the time is right.

The form in which the contact can take place can be varied. A quite common form of spiritual contact is by smell sensation. I was driving along in my car and went past the dog kennels from which we had obtained the family dog, now several years deceased. It made me think of him. I then had a "wet dog" smell sensation in my car, as if he were in the car with me, as he once had been on many occasions. No other dog had been in the car since his death, so I was curious why I experienced the smell.

My guide confirmed this was the spirit of my dog, who visited me often, but this was my first awareness of him. (For this contact to occur firstly one's pet must wish to visit you and secondly, the assistance of your guide is required). I have heard him subsequently in my mind. Now you know I am barking mad!

We had an enquirer who smells smoke sometimes, cigarette smoke or a pipe smoke. It travels with her. There is a perfume too. It is a Victorian type of perfume, violet or something similar. Her guide explained that in many of her incarnations she has had lives where she has used heightened senses. She has had spiritual lives before, and this is indicated by her search for meaning this time. Her guide believed she would recognise that she is on a kind of search for something, without really knowing what this is. She has the ability to sense spirit, and in her case, this sensing is in the form of smell or taste or hearing.

Her guide went on to explain that the particular smell of cigarette smoke that she notices around her, is when one who was close to her in a previous life visits her. This spirit was her husband previously; this was in a life in France, which she lived from 1874 to 1910. Her husband owned a bakery and it is his cigarette smoke she smells. He always smoked a particularly pungent brand.

Her guide further explained that the perfume is violet and is the perfume of her mother in a short life in England, during which she lived from 1860 to 1866. She died from influenza. They lived in York during that life and her mother was a seamstress. The then child, now the enquirer, was the only child her mother could have, having had a difficult labour and so being unable to have further children. This made the loss of her daughter so much more difficult for her. She and the child were close and it is her perfume that the enquirer can smell when she smells violet. (Mention of York prompted the relating of a déjà vu experience. The enquirer on visiting the city for the first time wanted to walk around the city wall. She felt at home there!)

We had another enquirer who asked if there is any way that she will know the presence of her guide, after we had confirmed his name as Michael and related that the last shared lifetime was in London in 1941, when they had both been killed in a German bombing raid on the capital. Michael said he could give several clues to her. He smoked Senior Service cigarettes and these she may sometimes smell. He wore cologne that smelled slightly of lavender and this may come through to her. He leaves a "feeling" of blue around her, which she may feel or even see, but mainly, she will feel a "presence" and know it to be him from her own intuition.

The enquirer went on to ask if the feeling she gets in the car is anything to do with Michael. She explained that she has a fondness for the car and has even given it the name of, not surprisingly, "Blue". Michael confirmed he is always in the car with her. The state that the human brain enters into when driving, is a condition akin to a state of deep meditation. This is because driving is done by one part of the brain while the rest can be thinking of something else completely. The phenomenon of arriving at a place without remembering the journey, being unable to recall passing a certain landmark or exiting a certain junction, explains it. Because of this, spirit often uses a car as a place for attempting contact, as the brain is in this receptive state.

Having discussed some of the forms and places of contact, how is it spirit finds us? One writer has given us the answer by saying that we each emit our own unique frequency. (*"Divine Intervention"* by Hazel Courtney). Although I am not a medium, I am able to distinguish the different vibrations of my more frequent spirit visitors (my guide and my mother).

I likened these unique frequencies to a telephone number. Our guide confirmed each spirit incarnated on Earth or elsewhere emits a frequency unique to itself. This frequency is carried through each and every incarnation of that spirit and is sometimes how spiritual thirds or actors in their play, find each other. Each is as unique to the spirit as a fingerprint is to a human. Spiritual contact is made by use of this frequency.

Under the heading of contact with spirit, the film, *"The Sixth Sense"* is worthy of reference. It portrays the sometimes frightening experience, of being a psychic child, although embellished with Hollywood graphics to make good cinema. Angela has memories of this herself, although not in quite the way shown in this film.

The film has many spiritual insights, however, some of which I spotted and now detail:

- ❖ The interview with the scriptwriter added to the video, revealed that he felt "guided"; he knew in advance the film would be a success and that Bruce Willis would star in it, even before he was approached.
- ❖ The child star actor was a prodigy (which I would attribute to a skill brought from previous incarnations).
- ❖ The film portrays the idea that ghosts are only wishing to communicate with us and that they are not in fact malevolent.
- ❖ What we consider as "evil spirit" is only man's interpretation and misunderstanding of the true reason and that when the reason is correctly understood, it can be seen that in fact, no evil exists in the spirit.
- ❖ Spirit will return to a place because of the trauma they underwent there when incarnated.

Life-plans, spirit guides, reincarnation, spirit contact, historical ghosts, trauma of place, all these topics in one film, making me feel less alone as a writer and hopefully providing a great stimulus to discussion for those who watched it.

Finally, before leaving this topic, the obvious question is "How can I have contact with my guide?" I am told that if one is not gifted with psychic powers, then do not look for quick results. The process can take some time, as there is a procedure to go through which should not be rushed. Learning to tune to your guide is not easy. The first essential is to clear your mind of the clutter and personal thoughts in order to create a space for the contact to take place. The means of doing this is a meditation.

There is no particular meditation script to use for this, use whatever helps you gain the best level of meditation. A tape is easier to use than a printed form, as the need to refer to a form breaks the meditative state. Sessions can be quite brief; it is not necessary to try to meditate for hours on end. Regularity is the key, however, do try and find some time on a daily basis, even if it is only ten minutes or so.

CRYSTALS

What is the function of crystals; are they a prop to communication or do they have unique properties? Crystals are used as props to channel spiritual communication, but it is the nature of the crystal that enhances the communication in this instance. This is a little different to the use of tarot cards, for instance. In the case of the cards, they are purely a prop to facilitate communication with the reader, the cards themselves have no properties to assist in this. With a crystal, however, the crystal itself is a little like an amplifier, it does not make spiritual contact exist where there is no predisposition for it to do so, but it does amplify communication where such communication exists.

So how do crystals help with spiritual healing or experiencing travel outside the body? The answer is that healing, spiritual travel and all other phenomena of this kind are the same as spiritual communication. Let me try to explain this statement. When a person has the ability to communicate with spirit, what they really have is the ability to attune to the vibrations of their spirit guide and interpret the spiritual energy messages passed, the teachings, philosophy and so on.

When a person has the ability to heal, they are again tuning into the vibration of their spirit guide and using the energy to transmit spiritual healing. When a person travels outside of the body, they are yet again tuning into the vibrations of their spirit guide and using the energy as a mode of travel. It is all the same energy, it carries all of these things and others within it; it is just a question of what is required of it at a given time. Just as a crystal acts as an amplifier for communication, it can act as an amplifier of the healing energy or the energy to travel. It is not that the crystal has a healing property, but rather that it can enhance or amplify healing that is transmitted from spirit.

ALTERNATIVE THERAPIES

As this is an important point, and one on which the understanding of so much else depends, I would like to summarise once again, the mechanics of mediumship, alternative therapies and the role of spirit guide.

In every case, without exception, a medium, healer or alternative therapist receives their communication from their **own** guide, their other third. They may see and hear a different voice, the one of the entity they are attempting to contact, but it is channelled through their own guide. *"There are no exceptions to this, it is the natural law"*, said our guide. Just as we in the human condition breathe oxygen, there are no exceptions to this; it is "the way of it" for all spiritual contact no matter what form it takes, there are no exceptions.

The mediums may not know this themselves; they may think they speak directly to various entities. They may not, indeed in most cases will not be aware of the structure of things. Because of its importance, our guide wished to repeat again, the only spirit contact is from the guide of the enquirer to the guide of the medium. There are no exceptions, even if the medium is not aware of this and thinks that they speak to a variety of spirits. They may see the entity from which the message comes, they may hear the voice, a different voice to that of their own guide, but it will be transmitted only by their own guide and come from the guide of the enquirer. If a medium says to you, "I do not work that way", they do, and they just do not know that they do. It is the only way possible. I apologise for belabouring this point, but it is fundamental and much misunderstood.

This truth holds good for all mediums, channels, psychic artists, dowsers, tarot readers and the rest. It also holds good for healers and all those treatments covered by the umbrella name of alternative therapies, those using Reiki, reflexology, regression therapy, crystal healing and all the other forms of healing treatment springing up on our planet that deal with the balancing of the body or similar. All of these practitioners are using spiritual healing, just as an actual healer uses it. Again, they may not know it, indeed in most cases will not know it, but they are all using the same thing, it is just the mode of operation that is different. Just as some mediums need a prop, tarot cards, flower reading, sand reading, psychometry, pendulum dowsing and all the rest, in order to receive a contact with spirit, so a healer may need a particular discipline with which they are comfortable in order to channel the healing.

Again, all these healers are receiving the healing from the guide of the patient, channelled through their own guide and administered by whichever mode they feel comfortable practising. They just don't know it. All the people using props such as tarot cards, flower reading, sand reading, psychometry, crystal ball and all of the other methods are mediums working from guide to guide, they just don't know it. Our guide corrected himself, as he should have said here, all the genuine people. He is afraid that in both mediumship and healing we will find the charlatans, those seeking only money or glory and with no ability to offer. These people do untold harm to the progress of spiritual recognition; they provide the sceptics with ammunition and sow seeds of doubt in those who wish to grow.

NIGHT TEACHINGS

Our guide related that through the night, spirit feeds information to us all, to our subconscious to be exact. For this, you are open and receptive in sleep. This again is a natural state that occurs, you do not need to do anything to let it happen. You may think you have reached a conclusion from a dream; you may not even be aware of the new information, or it may rise to the surface later when a topic is discussed and you won't realise how you know it or have that opinion. On waking, however, and if possible before you rise for the day, it is advisable to close down as detailed next.

CLOSE DOWN

Closing down your receptiveness, stops you being affected by any negativity you encounter in your daily routine and it also prevents others drawing energies from you without you actually allowing it. Some people have a draining effect without realising that they do; some may actively seek to draw others' energies from them, either consciously or subconsciously. If you have "shut down", should you encounter such a person, it will not have an effect on your health or energy levels.

To close down, advised our guide, use visualisation. It is not yet understood what a powerful tool visualisation can be. "*You are beginning to use it now, the members of your group, but generally, your race does not understand the power of visualisation,*" said our guide. (His mention of "group" refers to a group of five of which we are part, who work with natural earth energies in Lincolnshire).

Before rising, focus on the fact that you are open and in a receptive state. Angela always says 'thank you' for what may have been received through the night, then visualises a large glass dome shape, *"similar to those that cover skeleton clocks"* she says. In her imagination, she lowers this dome on burgundy red silken ropes until it covers her completely. Then she imagines herself walking around the dome on the inside of it, placing a burgundy cord along the rim at the level of the floor, *"like a draught excluder"* she says. She then visualises herself sitting down, cross-legged in the middle of it, safe and secure.

She leaves her spiritual self there while her material self deals with the day. If she works spiritually during the day, she just lifts off the dome before starting. She now has this so pat, that she can do it all in a matter of seconds and does not need to spend too long doing it. It is also a natural reaction to her; she does not even need to think about it. When she sits to work for an enquirer, she visualises the burgundy ropes returning and lifting off the dome to allow full and uninterrupted reception. This method may not be comfortable for everyone, but choose something similar, a blanket, a cloak, whatever feels right. Do pay attention to detail, however, the more detail you can add to the visualisation, patterns, colours, method and so on, the more effective it is, added our guide.

FAIRIES

An enquirer asked if there is any truth to the myth of fairies. We in turn, asked the "cosmic encyclopaedia", our guide. If we are honest, we expected an outright no, so were more than a little surprised when the question received the following answer. Our guide related that these are not true in the sense that they are portrayed in our myths and legends and in fairy stories. There is a phenomenon that has given rise to the legend, however, and he explained this to us as follows:

Certain spirit entities are charged with the design of species, and of all life, flora and fauna on all of the planets. These are members of the Council (more about this in chapter nine). They control all, so when scientists produce a new fruit or cross breed a new species, it is designed that this will occur and written into their life-plan that they will be the one to introduce it. This is a very simplistic overview of a complex subject, but serves for this purpose.

Spirit Council is also responsible for the placing of the ley-lines and the energy rivers on our planet, and indeed on every other planet. It is responsible for the feeder tubes that nourish the lines, and every aspect governing the development (or otherwise) of every planet. They will not clear a line or river that is blocked or soured by man's intervention nor do they govern the use of them, but they are the architects, the designers of all.

From time to time the entities that are charged with this may visit a planet. This they will do for what we will describe as a fact-finding mission, again a simplistic explanation for a complex subject. This is not done by means of an incarnation; they do not need to live out a life-plan for this task. It is not as a visitor from another planet where they might have an incarnation either. It is not as a "ghost", which is an entity remaining from an incarnation. This is different; it is a spiritual visit of limited duration by the spiritual entity.

They do not make contact with our race; they wish to be unobserved and to carry out the reason for the visit and leave. Just as our guide can visit the planet and "appear" to Angela if he so wishes, as well as communicating with her from the spiritual dimension, these entities can either work from spirit or visit the planet. Our guide asked us to remember that a council entity is a joined "Three"; to remember that there is no incarnated third for a council member, and so there is no route of contact under the normal laws.

Because of this, a visit usually goes unobserved by those of the planet, but there have, more so in the past than now, been those who could see these entities, or at least, sense them. If seen, they were usually observed as lights, but in some cases, if they deemed it correct, they would allow themselves to be seen with form by those of an advanced understanding or those who worked with energies. This gave rise to the legend of fairies, which has been embellished and distorted over the ages. Such visits are still occurring, of course, but those with the ability to see the entities are so far fewer than among the ancients. As these visits were always for a reason of nature, this has become incorporated into the myth too; hence we have stories of fairies with names from nature.

SELF-HEALING

We were asked if this was possible and if so, how to do it. The following is our guide's reply.

"In order to do this, sit and enter the state of meditation. Visualise a bright white light, like a laser beam, above you and entering through which ever of the chakras is closest to the problem. Direct the light through you to the source of the problem. Allow it to radiate there, changing from white to green (or whatever colour you feel will assist the problem), and back again, fluctuating in colour. Hold the visualisation for as long as possible and then consciously let it retreat back the way it came, don't just switch off in mid-stream, go through the process of allowing it to retreat."

He further commented that Angela has an excellent publication on the use of various colour, *"Know Yourself Through Colour"* by Marie Louise Lacey, one that is quite accurate, as they are not all so. He advised that in this, too, we should use own intuition and not rely on printed material alone. Our intuition will not lead us astray in matters such as this, commented our guide.

I would like to comment here more generally about the power of thought. Thought is the most powerful tool open to the human race. In spirit all is thought, the very dimension in which spirit exists is thought, all appearance, all possessions, everything is thought! I have referred in my first book, to the film *"What Dreams May Come"*. Not fully accurate in all aspects, but it gives the basic idea.

On Earth, too, if one could free oneself of doubts, of the scientist's need to see, feel and touch, to distrust and disbelieve anything that they cannot fully explain, if one could free and expand the mind to the degree that is done in spirit, then yes, one could create with one's thoughts. To some degree our race does this, but not in a meaningful way. Our thoughts create the difference between people. Our thoughts create superiority and inferiority. Our thoughts create political difference, war and turmoil. Our thoughts could create peace, harmony, joy and equality if they were allowed to do so.

MORE ABOUT GUIDES

I conclude this chapter with additional material about the guides and their interaction with us during the lifetime. Angels are spirit guides. The popular human conception of them as radiant celestial beings, with wings and halos, playing harps and singing in angelic chorus is the earthly misconception. Again, myth has interfered with reality. When spirit guides appear to those in the physical, they are often surrounded by their aura, which appears to those incarnated as a glowing, radiant light. This has fostered the idea of the halo of light.

The wings can be explained too; again, spirit guides, when they appear to those incarnated, often appear floating just above ground level, or even higher. This has given birth to the idea that these beings must have wings. Many do receive beautiful, spiritual vibration with the visitation, which could be attributed to angelic chorus. So yet again, time, myth and man's urgent need to turn into the mystical anything that he cannot readily explain or insist on closing his minds to, has done the rest.

Many that see and work with angels, do in fact, manifest the vibration of the spirit guide as a vision of the preconceived idea of an angel. This is not viewed as a problem; the fact that the vibration is felt, that the beauty, peace and harmony is felt, this is what matters. Appearance is of no importance to spirit, we can interpret it as we wish and so if our wish is to see an angel, then it is quite permissible that we do so. The only point to make is to know that this is really a spirit guide.

Having described an angel, do we have one each, are several looking over us, or different ones during our lifetime? Angela did mediumship for one who had attended an "angel workshop" and had an "angel reading". The practitioner had given her a list of angels that were with her, and the various attributes of each. This puzzled Angela, who understood that we only had our own guide with us at all times, and may on occasion have a spirit who has an interest in our welfare too; one who has shared the earthly incarnation and returned to spirit for instance, or one from the collection of preferred spirit spoken of earlier.

The explanation from our guide was that the "angels" seen in these readings are one's own guide, any of the above "extra" entities who may currently have an interest in one's welfare, or may be the practitioner picking up on past incarnations of the guide. As we have said, the guide always uses the persona of the last shared incarnation, but in the background of his or her vibration, will be every other incarnation he or she has shared with the incarnated one. This is what is sometimes interpreted as "angels that are with you". Angela was able to clarify for the enquirer that several of the names given to her were in fact previous shared incarnations with her guide.

So how would we define the role of a guide? A guide has as his or her foremost concern the life-plans of his incarnated two thirds. He knows all that is occurring in their lives at all times. He knows their every thought, their every action without the need to see. Immediately it is necessary for him to try and guide them or to plant the correct thoughts within their mind, he is with them. At other times, he is not required to be completely with them, but is still aware of all that is occurring with them.

(Whoops! Need to rewind and delete a few expletives having discovered that! In *"Macbeth"*, when his erstwhile trusted Cawdor is executed for treason, the Bard has the King say, *"There's no art to find the mind's construction in the face"*. Guides experience no such deception!).

How often does the guide communicate and can communication be two-way traffic? It is not wrong to meditate for an answer to one's own inner problems and questions as many think. It is in fact the ideal tool for communication with your guide who has your life-plan success at heart. Your guide will communicate with you at various times, whether you meditate or not. A guide will plant a seed of a thought in your mind if he finds you going off track or if he thinks you need a pointer to a certain topic. Things are dropped into our path at certain points throughout our lives.

Thoughts that concern daily living, "What shall I have for breakfast?" for example, or "What is the best way of dealing with a client's problem at work?" will be all your own thoughts (usually!). Others can be part you and part guide, where to go on holiday, for example, when to end a relationship or whether or not to emigrate. Other thoughts can be your guide alone, particularly if you are surprised at having the thought! In my own case, the suggestion to undertake a distance learning degree was my guide's initiative, which I then turned over in my mind and built upon the idea.

Guides may also be called to talk to others or to meet returning spirit where there has been a strong past life connection. They may assist lower level spirit in their life review or with their forthcoming plan. There are also many other tasks that have not even been discussed between our guide and ourselves. But through all of this, the minute their incarnated thirds require their input, they are there with them. This is instantaneous, like the blink of an eye. Remember, too, that what is a day, a week, a month or even a year to us, is but a flicker of time to a guide.

The closeness of a Three was illustrated when our guide gave us a list of abilities governed by spiritual level. We all knew instinctively the item on that list that would excite my curiosity and Angela's (Spirit Council!). Our guide knew it when he gave it to Angela, she knew it when she typed it and of course, I was immediately focused on it when reading it. We are all in tune with each other, we know to a great degree how each other thinks and acts, even if we both are not always consciously aware of it. This is natural in spirit, but is evidence of the degree of progression that we have both attained, that we have carried it into incarnation. The ultimate achievement is complete telepathy, but that is for masters.

This awareness of each other is a similar bond to that experienced by twins, as discussed in my first book. We are three parts of one whole, just as identical twins are two parts of one whole. This very fact means that in many ways we will be alike in our tastes, humours and thinking, as we indeed are.

Occasionally the feeling a guide has for his incarnated third can be transmitted. The love of a third is a mix of every type of love, the parental love, the love of a brother or sister, the love of a life-partner, the love of a friend, as your third your guide will have been all of these to you. All of these types of love combine to create a special emotional bond between the two, and we are advised by our guide that it is a great delight to spirit when it is felt by the incarnated third.

I can now explain why I felt a "high" after two important life-changing decisions I made in the past (both experienced incidentally whilst driving). My guide was communicating his pleasure at my decision, as it was the correct one for my life-plan.

These were leaving "safe" employment for uncertain self-employment, and secondly the decision to end my marriage unless my wife changed her attitude towards me, which she didn't.

Having revealed the fact that the guide knows his third's every thought, does he know the thoughts of his thirds alone, or through other guides, the thoughts of others, I wondered? Our guide replied that a guide only knows of his own knowledge the thoughts of his other incarnated thirds. However, if he needs to know the thoughts of another, one for instance that is affecting the lives of his thirds, then the other's guide will share his knowledge openly and willingly of his third's thoughts. He allows the thoughts of his third to be known so that the plans can come together. So, yes a guide may know the thoughts of others, but only through their own guide. He only has his own direct knowledge of his own third's thoughts.

For those in spirit already, there is open sharing of knowledge and of thought. It is only those in the incarnated state whose thoughts are only accessed by their own guide, but once accessed, these thoughts will be offered openly by the guide for general use for the good of all if required to be so. There are no secrets in the spirit state, nor is there any need for there to be; all is shared for the overall good. Our guide hoped this explained the subtle difference between knowing of a guide's own knowledge and knowing because all is known and shared in the spirit state.

This sharing of thoughts helps to explain, for example, how certain books come one's way at certain times. When a guide seeks to put works that will further your knowledge into your path, he just sends out the thought of what he wishes you to "discover", and he is made aware of the work required for the point, if he is not already aware of it himself. The author may or may not already be returned to spirit, but the content of his work will be known to his guide as it emanated from his own thoughts, so his guide will send your guide knowledge of it when he knows it is what is sought. Your guide formulates the question and the answer arrives by transference of thoughts.

There are two practical consequences following these revelations about guides that I can describe from my own experiences. The first is that guides can give you a mental push into an action you may have been thinking over, but held back from performing for various good reasons of you own. All of a sudden, you feel a compulsion to do it, even though a good part of you does not wish to, almost like the involuntary action of vomiting but minus the unpleasantness, you don't want to do it, but you can't help yourself. Where the person needs to do something to assist the plan, then guides can "kick-start" when the person is stalled.

This compulsion one friend of ours has named "Roger's involuntary urge". She had an important decision to make over the future of her business. She was aware of her guide's presence in the room and felt a compulsion to pick up the telephone and make an appointment with an adviser to arrange putting it up for sale. No more hesitation, she experienced my "involuntary urge". (Before criminal defence lawyers leap on this spiritual excuse for behaviours, please note no other person was harmed or injured in this illustration).

Another incident I can relate concerns a schoolteacher who had suffered stress to such a degree that she became ill and unable to work. A colleague invited her back to the school for a minor non-teaching purpose. Her instinct was to refuse. Despite not feeling too well, she felt a compulsion to get dressed, drive over and carry out the task. Once back at the school, some pupils recognised her and expressed their joy. She then realised her future lay in teaching, even if not in that environment and the visit's purpose was to steer her back to it, so that she did not choose an alternative career.

The second practical consequence is that I am aware of occasions when I have said something, my lips have moved and sound emitted, but afterwards I immediately thought, "Where did that come from?" "Did I really just say that?" Guides can collude to get one person to say a particular thing to another incarnated spirit (unbeknown to both of course); the guide's motive will be to assist your own or that third party's play.

An example of this was a friend who was hesitating about a change of job. He rang me about another matter and happened to say he was in the middle of typing his resignation letter, but was unsure about it. I instantly told him to just make a decision and reminded him there was no such thing as a "wrong" one. He finished his resignation letter. Our guide later confirmed my friend's own suspicions that his guide had spoken to mine because he was wavering and needed a push! Talk about being pawns in a game!

Most importantly, don't forget our guides love us! When in spirit, we do not have emotions in the sense of our human emotions. We do not know anger, irritation, resentment, hatred, revulsion, disgust, abhorrence, anxiety, fright or any other negative type of emotion. We do feel love, in all its forms, and in forms not accessible to us in the human condition. It is the whole purpose of spirit, to have examples of love through its many incarnations. As these experiences are gathered, so to is the capacity to send forth the feeling of love to those incarnated. This is a message we relayed from one guide to an enquirer.

"I wish to send my deep and encompassing love to you. I am deeply moved by your struggle to find yourself, and wish you to know that whenever you need to find inner peace, to relax and rejuvenate yourself, you will feel me with you; you can wrap yourself in my warmth and care, and feel my presence around you, caring for you always. I have a deep pride in your achievements as a person and I am confident and excited with the thought that you will achieve your destiny for our mutual benefit."

As the spiritually aware know, we are not alone! In our darkest moments, the despair can be the deeper because we think we are alone, that no one understands us, there is no one to turn to. What a comfort it is to know our guide is constantly with us, sending love when we need it.

Spirit only has for itself emotion of a non-negative nature. However, guides do "feel" all the emotion of their incarnated thirds, both good and bad, if they choose to do so. In times of great personal crisis, it is not unusual for those with awareness to feel the closeness of their guide who will be experiencing their emotion with them and trying to assist them to cope with it. In this way, the guide is better equipped to help with the life review when his thirds return to spirit, having had first hand experience of their feelings. Also, it helps the guide with his own progression, by allowing some understanding and growth to come from the incarnation of his thirds, even though he is the one staying "behind" on this trip!

So, in short, spirit can only experience emotion for itself of a non-negative form. Guides can never be disappointed or angry by the actions of their thirds, for instance. They can, however, feel these emotions acutely when they are experienced by the third incarnated. They feel it through them, it is not their own experience. They can feel joy at their third's achievements without feeling disappointment when they fail. This is because in spirit they are aware of the frailty of the human will and condition. Guides have no expectations of us, they are delighted when we take our intended path, but it is joy for us, not for themselves.

In the next chapter, I would now like to revert to a human level, and look at the spiritual explanation for some major life experiences.

CHAPTER EIGHT

MORE FROM THE MEDIUMSHIP CASEBOOK

I was excited to put together this chapter. It gives personal illustrations of the fundamental concept of life-plans introduced in my first book, *"Why Come Back?"* and helps to further explain why we return to human form.

This chapter takes quite a different view of man's life from conventional wisdom and looks at the spiritual perspective of some of the main experiences, from trauma linked to birth itself to so-called death. It gives instances of life-plans at work. In their explanation spirit is allowing the information to be given during the lifetime, rather than waiting for the review on return to spirit. The questions that have been answered include ones otherwise unfathomable and inscrutable.

In posing their questions the enquirers have felt in some way there was more to their experiences than met the eye. As the Great Poet remarks in *"Hamlet"*,

> *"There is something in this more than natural, if philosophy could find it out."*

I offer you the spiritual philosophy received in answers to these points put to us by various enquirers:

- ❖ Why did my mother die while giving birth to me?
- ❖ Why did I have to endure the loss of my baby while still in the womb?
- ❖ Why was my baby born prematurely?
- ❖ Why did I become an orphan?
- ❖ Why was I given up for adoption?
- ❖ Why did my biological parents treat me so coldly?
- ❖ Why is my sister so unloving?

- Should I forgive my father?
- Why is my daughter violent?
- Why have I had an overweight problem since childhood?
- Why do I view the occupants of wheelchairs as fortunate?
- Why am I terrified when I see someone drunk?
- Am I responsible for my husband's drinking problem?
- Why am I suffering from ME?
- Why is my mother bed-ridden?
- Why do I have difficulty breathing and have little sense of taste or smell?
- Did I do the right thing leaving my old employer?
- Am I in the right occupation?
- Why am I attracted by Greek and Roman statues?
- Did I have a near-death experience whilst giving birth?
- Was I wrong to feel joy at a family funeral?

I have added two questions of my own:

- Is the soul indestructible?
- Should we be concerned about genetically modified plants and embryos?

PARENTAL DEATH AT BIRTH

We had an enquirer whose mother died giving birth to her. The enquirer herself was starved of oxygen during the birth and this left her with a disability, which has caused her to struggle in life. She has tried to go forward with everything but feels that she has been held back. She asked if her guide could tell her the reasons for this and the reason for the death of her mother please?

He replied that when the life-plans for both she and her mother were designed, they both chose these traumas in their lives for the spiritual growth obtainable. Her mother had chosen to learn the lesson of love taught by the carrying of a child but not having the satisfaction of raising that child. The level of love for the unborn child is not fully understood – many think that the strongest bonding comes from the birth, but this taught the lesson that the love that can begin before the birth can be just as strong a love. Her mother has been drawn to an interest in her daughter's life from that time until she reincarnated.

The enquirer chose to suffer the disability and to grow up without her mother to nurture her, for the lesson of learning that even in the face of adversity, it is possible to rise to one's own goals. The challenges posed by this double tragedy so early in life has strengthened her character and made her the person she is in this life. Her guide advised she has progressed spiritually far more than she realises in this incarnation and will realise, on return to spirit, how well she has done in this life despite its hardships and pitfalls.

There were further consequences arising from this event, in that the enquirer continually felt dominated by her father. The cause, her guide explained, was that her father always felt a sense of inadequacy following the death of her mother. He was a proud and stubborn man and had mixed feelings following her loss. He felt cheated by life, inadequate because he had been unable to prevent her death, guilty because he had been instrumental in creating the pregnancy that bought it about, quite irrationally resentful towards his wife for leaving him with the child, and confused because he was used to having his way, to being obeyed, and in this he was thwarted. This cauldron of mixed emotions affected his attitude to his daughter. Deep down, he transferred some of these emotions into his relationship with her said her guide, so completing his analysis from spirit. To which I might add on an earthly level, another cross she chose to bear!

STILLBIRTH

This enquirer had lost a baby in 1999 when she was six month's pregnant. The baby died in the womb and she had to go through the trauma of labour knowing there would be no baby at the end. Could her guide further explain this please? He answered by firstly reminding her that the child chooses the parents it wishes to be born to. It chooses parents that will provide in their own life-plans, the circumstances it requires to fulfil its plan.

Having said this, the soul attaching to the baby at that time required only to experience life in the womb. It required the experience of connecting to the mother in this state; of experiencing the mother's emotions and feeling the love projected towards her, the unborn baby. Having received the experience required for her spiritual fulfilment in that incarnation, she did not need the birth experience and so returned to spirit. She has reincarnated again as a girl child already, with a new plan this time.

    She chose this enquirer as a parent because it was in the enquirer's life-plan to suffer the emotions of this experience and to reinforce the lesson of loss and love of one no longer with you. She also experienced the love she felt for this child without ever even knowing it, a different aspect again. Her guide continued by saying that it may make it easier to know that the child was not deprived of life, but actually fulfilled her destiny in this way. She was thankful to her mother for providing the experience. They will continue to have a bond, even though she has reincarnated.

    There is a further revelation connected to this event. We noted in the case of Cheryl, who similarly experienced a stillbirth, that the spirit did not later reincarnate as a subsequent child. Happily, the spirit did so in this instance, which of course, explains the last comment about having a bond, even though she has reincarnated. Her guide believed that the enquirer had always known this. The two children even have a resemblance, or would have done, had the baby chosen to take earthly incarnation, he confirmed. This explained why mother and child experience a special bond between them, a kind of telepathy.

    The enquirer went on to make the connection that they were spiritual thirds. Their lives have thus a great part to play in the plan of each other, as indeed do all incarnated thirds. The first instance of stillbirth is an illustration of how thirds impacting on one another is not necessarily always joyous, it may be sorrowful, but whatever the emotion, it will have spiritual progression as its motive.

    Angela raised the point that we had previously been told that both incarnated thirds must return to their spirit state and to their third who remained in spirit, so that all three may be together to plan the next incarnation, and that one incarnated third cannot return to spirit and reincarnate again until the other is back too. This being the case, how was it that the baby could reincarnate before the mother returned?

Our guide explained that the experience of the stillbirth and the rebirth to the same mother who was her third, were both part of the same life-plan, rather than two separate events. This had been planned by both of them before the mother incarnated, so was not a new plan for the baby. This can only occur if both mother and baby are thirds, and the baby can only be reborn to the same mother for it to be part of the same event.

If the baby had not died in the womb but been born alive, even if she had only survived for a few minutes, then this would be a complete event. The baby would indeed need to wait until the mother, her third, returned to spirit before incarnating again in those circumstances. The factor determining that the baby in the actual stillbirth can reincarnate to the same mother as part of the same plan, is that a stillborn baby does not take independent life, even for a few seconds.

PREMATURE BIRTH

Still with the same enquirer, a further twist to the plot was that this second baby was premature, so much so that she struggled to survive. Could her guide explain why this was, please, when she had already learned the anguish of loss?

He answered that, for the spirit that is now her child, the fight for survival after being born prematurely was the next natural step following her previous lesson from life only in the womb. To be born and then to struggle to retain life formed the one part of this child's life-plan. Together they had planned that this would provide the enquirer with the lesson of love learned from anxiety and anguish over a child, made even more acute by the fact of having lost her before and the bond made between them. This again was all part of the lesson of this life for the two of them that they devised in spirit. This anxiety also strengthened the bond between the anxious parents and served in this way to provide for a variety of life-lessons in their life-plans, concluded the guide. What a tangled web we sometimes weave for ourselves!

ORPHANED

When I reveal this same enquirer was orphaned at the age of thirteen, you might begin to wonder where all this bad luck originated. Her spirit's wish to hasten its spiritual progression is the reason. While it may be viewed as bad luck and a disastrous life on Earth, when returned to spirit, her successful negotiation of it will be a huge success, resulting in a spiritual leap forward.

She lost both her mother and father at a young age to heart attack. This left her aged thirteen and her sister aged nine. Her stepfather brought them both up following her mother's death. Could her guide explain why this was please?

In my first book, I explained generally the situation regarding the choosing of parents, the forming of life-plans and the reasons behind them. Her guide explained that in this life, she and her sister had planned the life in which they would be left at a young age without parental support. A difficult concept in human terms perhaps to embrace, but not so from a spiritual perspective, growth coming from challenges overcome.

Her guide continued by saying that this enabled them to experience the coming to terms with grief, and the lesson of learning that it is still possible to love when the object of the love is no longer available to you. They learned many lessons in their formative years from this tragedy. They experienced the care of one not a biological parent, and learned to be self-sufficient at an early age. Although the time was trying for them both, they actually grew by the experience of bereavement in a way that is not usually learned until much later in life. The lesson of valuing what you have while you have it has also been learned.

This provides an illustration of the teaching point that our children are only our children biologically. One can receive as great a degree of care, greater in some cases, from someone without a biological connection, but who is connected to you spiritually.

The comparison with one of my own past lives (India 1480-96) comes to mind here as a similar experience. As I have said previously, the older the spirit, the more difficult the life, usually.

ADOPTION

Another life situation that fits well at this point is to consider adoption from a spiritual viewpoint. We have discussed the fact that we choose our biological parents; similarly we choose adoptive parents.

We had an enquirer who wished to understand why if we pick our parents, did the parent she picked have her adopted? Her guide responded by explaining that when life-plans are made, many things are taken into account. Parents are chosen whose own life-plan enhances your own. A spirit may choose to be stillborn for instance as in the earlier example, just experiencing life in the womb. For this they will need to choose a parent who has in their life-plan to have a stillborn child.

In this enquirer's case, she decided in this life, to learn the lessons supplied by being given up for adoption and having a life with adoptive parents. For this, she chose a parent who had in her plan to learn from the trauma of having to give up a child. All lessons are ultimately to teach about love in its many forms. This particular scenario provides many lessons on the subject for all the players.

"Remember," said her guide, *"to understand light, you need to experience dark. To understand heat, you need to know what cold is. You have to understand the negative to understand the positive"*. The choice of parent served the enquirer in her life this time, although she will not really understand this fully until she returns to spirit herself.

A further teaching point arose by looking at this same event from the situation of the biological father. The enquirer wished to know if her biological father ever knew she existed. Her guide answered that he did know about her mother's pregnancy and her birth. He eventually found out from another, not from her natural mother. He knew she existed, but by this time was married to another.

His pain through life was that he was unable to have a child with his wife but knew that he had this child that he could not see, could not even acknowledge, as he had to keep the secret. His wife suffered from a feeling of inadequacy over the inability to have a child and would have felt herself to be even more inadequate, had she known about the illegitimate child. He was a caring man, and would not hurt his wife more by telling her this. Also, because of the time, the propriety of the age, he would not have compromised the natural mother by contacting her about this, knowing that she had gone to lengths to keep the secret, even at the cost of great emotional pain to herself.

Not only did this lady experience adoption, she also experienced the death of her adoptive father when she was only aged six. When as an adult, her natural mother died, she attempted to go to the funeral. She experienced rejection by the rest of the family, who still wished the secret to be kept, even after death. This naturally caused hurt and she asked why this happened.

Her guide explained that in her plan this time she chose to experience at first hand the closed minds of those living insular lives, in small, closed communities. The reason for the rejection was rather involved. First, and as in so many earthly situations, money was at the route of the trouble. There was concern in this regard by some who feared open acknowledgement of her would lead to problems over her estranged mother's estate. Others were afraid that the truth would finally out, and that the stigma would attach to them, even at this late stage. All these things are unimportant in life really, and should be seen in perspective.

The enquirer, feeling this pain, will now understand the depth of it and realise the inhumanity that one person or group can inflict on another without ever a blow being struck; will understand that emotional pain can be as damaging as physical, and will in many cases last longer. These persons should be pitied for their inability to extend love to others. It shows the degree of spiritual growth needed in this area, concluded her guide. That concerns over money and appearances were held as more important than the feelings of another human being provided exactly the lesson she had set out to learn from it, the level of closed mindedness of people living in these small communities.

A DYSFUNCTIONAL FAMILY

I now describe three enquiries under this heading.

1. We had an enquirer whose sister is causing problems within the family. She does not speak to the enquirer and is causing trauma to their father. Could her guide explain why, please?

He answered that her sister is undergoing a difficult incarnation this time. In fact, she has been stuck in this particular loop for her last two lives. She is having difficulty with the family relationship situation, is unable to give anything of herself to others in her family circle. In the family situation, the lessons to learn on Earth are of giving a part of oneself to others in the family group; being one's own person, but being completed by other family members. As part of the lesson, we also experience bad family relationships in some lives, in order that we may understand and appreciate the good.

Her sister, two lives ago, experienced a bad family situation. Her father of that life abused her, the eldest daughter. She had younger siblings that did not suffer in this way and resented them for this. She has carried through from that life, resentment to the life father and her siblings of the subsequent incarnations, being her last life and the current one. She is failing to realise that in this and the last incarnation, she is supposed to experience the love of the family unit. She is finding herself deliberately causing her own unhappiness, her own estrangement from her family. She is treating her father in the way she does without realising she is still seeking to punish the father she had two incarnations ago, not the current one.

Unfortunately, unless she sees the way of it for herself or attends a regression therapist who may assist her in reaching the root cause, she will not move on from this position again in this lifetime either. This will cause another repeat. (This lady is an illustration of the spiritual law that we repeat and repeat until we are successful. Time is not an issue in this.)

The guide went on to advise that the enquirer should not grieve for the loss of a sister's love. She should not assume any responsibility for their current relationship; the problem is her sister's to work out. She can be supportive to her father and hope by her positive action to undo some of the negative actions of her sister, but ultimately only the sister herself can make the change.

2. We had another enquirer with a problem father. She felt that if she were able to forgive her father for her childhood, she would

move on spiritually, but she seems unable to find it within herself to forgive him.

Her guide answered that it is not necessary for her to forgive; this is a difficult thing to achieve when one is injured from childhood. Better that she concentrate on understanding life-plan; that she realise her father is working through his own problem with love, and that he needs to be able to come to terms with his own inabilities in this life, or he will repeat again. He has now had four previous lives where he has failed to learn this lesson, and unless he manages to find revelation in later life this time, may need to repeat yet again.

Her guide further advised that if she can come to the realisation that this is her father's spiritual journey, his struggle, that he cannot help the way he is, it is in his life-plan to work through this problem, she might find herself less injured by his behaviour. She need not forgive him in order to move on, just come to the understanding of why he is this way and accept that this is his problem, and not one she need burden herself with. Such acceptance gives a lightening of one's own burden inflicted by the contact from such a relationship and allows one to move spiritually to the next level.

The enquirer did not elaborate on "problem father", so I am not certain if this referred to sexual abuse, but believe it may do. Guides respect confidentiality and will not offer Angela more information than the enquirer does, or further elaborate beyond answering the specific questions put to them.

We have heard a "past life therapist" speak of how she has dealt with the issue of parental abuse, by taking a person back to a life in which the abuse occurred. She had her client meet the spirit of her father from the life, so she could see that he was at core, a loving spirit, a being of light, and so come to understand he was not his real spiritual self in his behaviour towards her. He had chosen to learn lessons from his earthly incarnation that were served by the abusive behaviour. Such therapy does require care, with attention particularly being paid to "closure" of such a meeting. Unbeknown to the therapist, perhaps, the enquirer's spirit guide is closely involved to ensure all is well.

3. We spoke of one example of an antagonistic relationship between mother and son in Cheryl's life lessons. We had another

enquirer who does not have a good relationship with her daughter. They have good patches and bad, some even resulting in physical violence by the daughter towards her mother. This has been the case from her being a young child. Could her guide give an explanation please?

He replied that her daughter is quite a young spirit. She is new to the human condition and is not able yet to control or handle her emotions. She currently finds it easier to blame her mother for the ills of the world than to give her credit for anything. She has resented many of her mother's actions and decisions throughout life and needs to learn that love should transcend such things and not be based on selfish need.

In order to complete her plan this time, she needs to come to the realisation of the love that she has for her mother, which she does have even though she refuses to acknowledge it. She has designed her life-plan this time, so that she comes to realise this love late in her life, even if this is after her mother has returned to spirit, her guide further advised.

STAGE PROPS

Again, I give details of three enquirers under this heading.

1. The first prop is perhaps the body itself. In *"Why Come Back?"* I discussed the saying that "beauty is in the eye of the beholder" and the fact that we choose our bodies. We have not had anyone of extreme beauty, or lack of it, consult us, but we have had enquirers who have a personal struggle with body shape.

One gentleman enquirer had been plagued with problems relating to his weight since a child. Could his guide help explain this please? The answer given was that in this life, it was decided that he would choose to battle against a physical problem with his appearance, as a tool to learn one of his life-lessons. The problem of being overweight was chosen for this.

The lesson to be learned from such an appearance problem, is that a kind and loving nature can shine through and be appreciated by others, no matter what the outward appearance; physical appearance is not the thing to love, it is what is inside that counts. The enquirer has struggled to accept this, feeling that others, his peers particularly, will not like him, that females will not be attracted to him, because of his weight. In fact, with a kind and loving nature such as his, the right person will find the attractive thing about him and not judge him by his outward appearance.

"*Now*", continued his guide, "*when the weight is at last coming under control, he may realise this for himself. It has made him gentle in his handling of others with physical handicap, disability or appearance problems, and added to his kind and gentle nature. He no longer need feel at a disadvantage because of appearance, and in time will possibly come to realise that those who caused him pain over it, were not understanding human beings, were shallow in their own natures if they put physical beauty over beauty of soul*". This was one of the major lessons to be learned in this incarnation for him.

2. When we considered some of the life lessons for Eva, her problem with her legs in a past life and in the current one was discussed, as being a circumstance that worked well once, so was used again. We had an able bodied enquirer who had a peculiar response to wheelchairs. He views the occupants as almost fortunate. Could his guide offer an explanation?

He most definitely could, but not one he thought the enquirer would envisage. He went on to explain that in spirit, the enquirer had been involved on many occasions, with the planning of lives for others of lower spiritual level than himself. As we know, the higher the level of spirit, the more difficult the life-plan; it is also true that those suffering disablement, or severe or terminal illness, may obtain a huge leap of spiritual growth from the experience.

Within himself, the enquirer knows this and as such sees the positive aspects of the experience of severe disablement and realises that the sufferer may be fortunate in their spiritual life, to have this condition. He has experienced a life of disablement himself, which served him greatly in his spiritual progression and this is also deep in his memory and leads him to think of this as a fortunate situation.

The guide's explanation here may earn me some brickbats from certain quarters! I would refer the reader to Angela's disability experience that I discussed in *"Why Come Back?"* should anyone want further spiritual explanation for this circumstance.

3. Another illustration of a repeat scenario came to us with a lady enquirer, and concerned alcohol abuse. She first explained that when she sees anyone who is drunk, she finds herself in a state of terror.

Her guide gave the past life explanation for this. She had a life in Ireland from 1746 to 1781 during which she was the eldest child in a family of eight children. Her mother died in the birth of the last child and her father was a drinking man with a short temper. He was rough and brutal and had no care for his family. He abused both her and her sister, particularly when he was drunk, which he often was. Her sister ran away from home, but she stayed to care for her younger siblings, as she had promised her mother she would. She never married, her experiences with her father having prevented any possibility of a healthy relationship with men.

In her current life, her husband is a heavy drinker and she eventually withdrew from him, because of her feelings of extreme discomfort and agitation around him when he had been drinking. Her lady guide explained the spiritual reasoning for the repeat circumstance in a life. She explained that there are three ways a life such as the one above can affect a person.

First, if the plan for the past life was not met, for instance, if she had failed to remain and look after her siblings, she may have repeated the experience to get it right in a following life. However, she did meet the challenge so did not need to repeat the plan for this reason.

The second instance is that a particular set of circumstances can work well in the fulfilment of a lesson. This can lead one, once returned to spirit, to choose similar circumstances to assist in the creation of the spiritual lessons for subsequent lives. A little like a case of "it worked once, let's use it again."

The third possibility is a past life fingerprint, not intended to encroach on the current life, but one that does when the person finds themselves in contact with circumstances that precipitate the distant and unacknowledged memory. This is the answer in this instance. We have encountered it as an explanation in a number of other mediumship situations too.

In the current life, the enquirer had met a new partner. She had not sought to divorce her husband, but continued living in her matrimonial home and leading a separate life. Her husband had started to drink heavily again because of this. She was beginning to feel guilty and responsible and feared she had made a wrong decision; she wished to ask her lady guide if this was the case, or was her husband's problem his own to resolve?

Her guide responded by saying that the meeting of a new partner was absolutely planned. The effect this has had on her husband is his problem to work through. He is repeating a life in which addiction, or at least excess, formed a part. He did not succeed in his last incarnation, in conquering this and is repeating it in the hope of correcting it this time. The enquirer cannot take this task from him, he must be allowed to work through it in his own way. He needs this experience in order to progress through the spiritual levels.

She still felt a responsibility towards her husband and was concerned for his future life without her. Her guide had the following message for her:

"All spiritually advanced beings have a difficulty in feeling that they might be the cause of hurt in another. The task is to let go of this emotion and allow those around you to try and grow spiritually themselves. Your husband has yet to work through part of his plan. He is not spiritually advanced, and needs to learn certain lessons in order to progress. He needs to see that he is the cause of his own unhappiness, that he cannot blame others for what happens to him, but needs to take responsibility for his own life and not act the role of victim. To be proactive in his life rather than reactive.

We cannot give further details of what is in his life-plan, this is information only available to him, but of course, he would not seek it due to his level of progression. What we would say is that you should try to accept that whatever happens in his life is meant to happen for his own spiritual good. Staying with him out of pity or habit would deny him this, so you are actually being considerate of his needs by allowing him the opportunity to grow from this part of his life. You would naturally like him to have in his life what you have found in yours, but he is not spiritually capable of the experience, so it would not mean the same to him at this time, even if he were to have it."

I would add this was a specific answer and was addressed to an individual enquirer. It should not be read as a generalisation for all who are living with the problem of addiction in another. In other circumstances, the correct spiritual decision might be to stick with the problem, particularly where care of children is involved, as exemplified in the Irish past life.

I would also like to underline some of the words of wisdom here, especially the need for certain people to see that they are the cause of their own unhappiness, who blame others, fail to take responsibility for their own life, but prefer the role of victim. I have encountered such individuals, as I am sure many others will have done, too. Whilst I would like such persons to see in their lifetime the higher perspective, their spiritual level may mean their opportunity to do so will only happen on return to spirit.

In the case above, the lady was an older spirit and her husband a younger one. This point of recognising the sometimes large spiritual age differences in persons of close social or biological relationship was brought home to me recently. I had a surprising and in depth discussion on spiritual matters with the twenty year old son of one of my friends. I found it surprising, as his father and other family members have no spiritual leanings, and my contact with him in his youth would have led me to believe that he would not have, either. I should know by now not to be surprised at the family situations older spirits choose to incarnate into for the challenge it provides them, and this reinforced it to me.

Following the discussion, to my shock-horror, he remarked to his father, *"You are a young spirit with a lot to learn!"* Thankfully my friend didn't realise the depth of the remark, as I tried to hide under the table! I had earlier merely explained in our discussion that there were differences in spiritual ages between people, and this can be the explanation for the feeling of being out of sync with those in our immediate surroundings. On hearing that, the son instantly summed up his father! I pictured the son's guide having patiently waited twenty years to have the opportunity of saying that!

ILLNESS

Serious illness is a great fear for many of us. In *"Why Come Back?"* I related that all serious illness is an intended event, designed in a plan to precipitate spiritual growth. Not surprisingly, illness has featured in the questions of some enquirers. Here are three.

1. One lady was suffering from Myalgic Encephalomyelitis (ME). Her guide gave the following explanation. The ME she is experiencing has come about from the stress in her life. The underlying feeling of a gap in her relationship that she has felt for some time, together with the recent financial pressures, have combined to create the right chemistry within her for this to take hold.

The guide went on to explain to the enquirer that all major illnesses and accidents are planned before incarnation, for the experience they will give as an aid to spiritual progression. The guide could not tell her that she will ever be completely free of ME but she will experience remissions and her general symptoms will be less severe, when other elements of her life improve. The timescale for this was during the next three years from the time of the reading.

2. Another enquirer asked why her elderly mother had her stroke, making her bed-ridden and in need of daily nursing. Her guide replied by saying that her mother had always been a woman of strength, one who did not tolerate fools gladly. She was not a person who, in her younger days, showed patience or sympathy with the sufferings or misfortunes of others to any great degree. She did not suffer disability herself very often and could not empathise with those who did.

Now, as she realises more of her spiritual nature towards the end of her life, she is learning first hand about suffering and disability. The lesson is hers and was written into the plan for her. The enquirer is learning from association, but the lesson was not for her, it was intended for her mother, confirmed the guide.

3. Illness can have a past life origin, too. There are a number of popular books on this subject; in particular, the books by Dr Brian Weiss are worthy of a mention in this context. (One writer has

used the term "cell memory" for this phenomenon. That is not quite correct, as memories are within the soul. All cells renew themselves periodically, so could not memorise events.)

I now give an illustration that shows an instance of a psychosomatic mechanism at work. The enquirer suffers from difficulty breathing and has had a poor sense of smell and taste for some years.

Her lady guide explained that the problem she experiences is caused by the fingerprint of a past life which has encroached into the current one, and this is her body's response to the problem. She experienced a life in Sicily in the 1700s, when she lived in the shadow of Mount Etna. It erupted, and although she escaped the area, she inhaled the ash and fumes, which caused severe blistering of her nasal passages and throat. Following this, she never had a sense of smell or taste again.

Her guide further explained that in that life, at the time of the eruption, in which members of her family were killed, she was traumatised, frightened, knew worry, concern, terror, fear for her loved ones, a whole range of emotions. Following this cocktail of emotions, she was left with the problems to her throat and nasal passages.

What has occurred in many of her incarnations since this time, and again in this one, is that every time she experiences worry, trauma, fear or concern for her loved ones, an emotion of this type for any prolonged period, or of any strength, she is, unbeknown to herself, associating it with the result following that emotion in the past life, and is unwittingly expecting to have problems with her nasal passages.

The reoccurrence of this problem she was experiencing at the time she visited us, had been precipitated by her concerns over her son. It was unfortunate that this was timed to occur just as she embarked on a new business venture; even though she has had an inner excitement for the project, it had created additional pressures. The project itself would not have caused her any problem because of her enthusiasm and inner knowledge that it formed part of her destiny, but on the tail of her worries over her son, it has exacerbated the problem that had already set in.

Her guide went on to say that the enquirer could be free of this problem now that she knows the root of it. In meditation, she can acknowledge the facts of it, acknowledge that now she knows there is no reason to fear it any longer, and ask that it now be taken away as she no longer has a need of it. When she has happiness in other areas of her life, this task will be easier to perform.

Her guide concluded by saying that the long-term solution is for her to work on realising that this problem belonged to the other life. She needs to retrain her subconscious to realise that this response is inappropriate in this life. She should know that this is in no way the result of karma. She is not suffering for any karmic reason; she has simply brought through the memory, which is causing inappropriate reactions in this life.

OCCUPATION

Many enquirers ask if they are on the right path. Often they have sought mediumship from us when at a crossroads situation. As I have previously written, even if an incorrect choice is made, if it is an important crossroads for the life-plan, the guide will find ways to present it a second and even subsequent times, so that the intended decision is made, and the life-plan succeed. Again, I give three illustrations.

1. We had an enquirer, whom I shall refer to as David, who had almost inflicted a self-paralysis on himself and caused grief to his family because he was unsure of his destiny. He recognised he had no satisfactory future with his old employer and had eventually managed to take the step of changing job. Yet he was not comfortable in his new job, so much so that his performance was suffering. He had entertained thoughts of approaching his previous employer and asking for his old job back.

His guide had these words of wisdom for him: *"All David must do is keep an open mind and when an opportunity arises, recognise his internal feeling that this is the correct path to take"*. Trust in his own inner understanding was the lesson here, or in our terms, having the courage of his convictions. His feelings that maybe he should return to his old job, were the result of a wavering of these convictions, a seeking of comfort in the familiar. Inwardly he recognised that he would quickly return to the same frustrations that he had experienced and which had caused the initial move.

He has passed the first of the spiritual tests, by not approaching his old employer, even though the opportunity to do just that had presented itself quite neatly in the past week. His next spiritual test was to have the convictions and the trust to follow his destiny when it is presented to him. *"David will know, we are sure of this"*, continued both guides, *"he will know when he is on the correct path. The path will be presented, he can be happy in that fact. He is in the right place at this time, this is a means to an end, and as such, should be enjoyed for the experience it offers".*

The pop group *"Enigma"* has a North American Indian song, *"Return to Innocence"*, which includes the line, *"Just believe in destiny"* and that seems to summarise the message here. (Incidentally, according to a "Times" interview, the artist knew as a teenager that his career lay in pop music, much to his mother's consternation. Life-plan being accessed, no doubt!)

2. Another enquirer was an example of those with a spiritual destiny, should they choose to follow it. Her guide explained the position: *"She has a change of direction coming her way in the future, should she decide to follow it, but this is not for some time yet. She has ability, even if she is as yet unaware of it, to lift others, to take them out of themselves, to focus their concerns away from self and give them a wider base to focus on.*

This is a gift and should she follow a career that enables her to use it she will find satisfaction and fulfilment from the work, together with a degree of material success. She has reached a crossroads in her life at this time. A complete change of direction may involve training or additional learning, may involve a period in which she may seem to take a step backwards materially, but if she decides to follow the path which will be made clear to her, this will only be a temporary set back. She has a great future working with people, for their inner well-being. The opportunity for this will arise, she should watch carefully for it, if she decides that she wishes to follow her destiny."

3. Before leaving the topic of occupation, I will add a cautionary tale. An enquirer asked why Greek and Roman statues compelled her. Her guide answered with a past life reason in which she had a male incarnation as a sculptor, a Greek, who chose to work in

Rome and lived approximately 478-425BC. He never married in this incarnation, devoting his life to his art.

The lesson learned from this incarnation was that single-mindedness pursuit of a material goal, even an artistic one, which can enrich the soul of others, leaves one undernourished and unfulfilled spiritually. On return to spirit he realised that he had missed the opportunity to progress spiritually on several occasions by his single-minded pursuit.

Now that sounds familiar! The reader may recall my life as Enku in Japan, 1628-95, in which I failed the life-plan by allowing the pursuit of a task to become an obsession to the exclusion of the reason for undertaking it initially.

NEAR DEATH EXPERIENCE

An enquirer had what she believed to be a near death experience. During childbirth, she had a difficult time and was given morphine. She saw herself in the operating theatre before she actually arrived there. She also felt herself going into a tunnel and heard music. Could her guide tell her about this, she wondered?

He confirmed that she did have a near death experience, as she believed, and it was not the drugs causing hallucinations as others had suggested. He was sure deep down that she knows it was real. The tunnel of light which all go through when they first leave the body can appear either right next to the earthly body, or the spirit may need to rise up to find the tunnel. The spirit is drawn through the tunnel and, depending on the circumstances, may have the choice to go on or return. Differing things are experienced in the tunnel, some hear beautiful music, music different to anything heard on Earth, some feel a warmth and a feeling like being wrapped in a cloud, some hear a gentle, kindly voice, and there are other experiences that can be felt, too.

For those for whom it is the correct time, the journey through the tunnel is a one way street; others, who find themselves there may encounter a life crossroads and be given the choice of going on or returning; some are told that they must return, as it is not the correct time to go.

In this enquirer's case, her soul left the body due to the trauma of the incident. It should have remained near the body and re-entered when things were more stable. As she had recent memory of the "path home", once out of her body, she sought the tunnel automatically. Spirit however, knew that it was not time for her to go home at that time, she still had much to do, so she was allowed the refreshment to her soul of spending a little time in the tunnel, before they returned her to her earthly incarnation to complete her task.

Her liking of the colour yellow is, as she believes, from that time. This is something shared by my partner Angela, who had her own near death experience, which I described in *"Why Come Back?"*

DEATH

I began the chapter with the subject of untimely death. More frequently as we ourselves age, the funerals of friends, family and work colleagues impact on us. Death is a birthday of course, in spiritual terms; one has returned home. Very few of us experience bereavement in those terms, however!

We did have an enquirer, an older spirit, who saw the spiritual perspective of death, but was berated by his wife for not grieving as he should for the loss of his father and sister. His guide gave the following message.

"You were exactly right to feel joy at the passing of your sister and father. When a spirit leaves the Earth plane having completed their life-plan and achieved their desired lessons, it is right to celebrate for them. It is only the self-serving part of the human animal that feels sorrow; this is most often sorrow for their own loss and not based on the feelings of the departed one. It is yet again a mark of an incarnated older spirit, to understand the joy of returning to spirit, and to celebrate for them in the face of one's own loss. You were absolutely right in your feelings about this, and should not be diverted by the thoughts of others."

These are not remarks to be appreciated by those who have not reached the same spiritual age. I certainly grieved deeply and at length for the loss of my mother. That was before I had spiritual beliefs; clearly the enquirer in this case had them earlier in his life.

AFTER DEATH

This might be a suitable point to ask the question, is the soul indestructible? Some people die in extremely violent circumstances, so does the soul always survive? My guide confirmed that the soul always survives. The human body is a vessel; it matters not what happens to the vessel, the contents are preserved. No matter how hideous the death, on the moment that life is extinguished, at exactly that moment, literally with the drawing of the last breath, the soul leaves the body and returns to its spiritual state. Immediately any deformity, physical trauma, any disfiguration or mutilation is gone, the soul is complete and unaffected.

Speaking of the soul prompted a further question concerning the topic of genetically modified plants and animals, and the possible effect on the soul. Much criticism is being voiced about the ethics of this development, yet surely no amount of genetic engineering will affect the soul?

Our guide answered and reiterated that every single thing that lives, lives only as a vessel for the soul, bearing in mind the past information I have given about the difference between the soul of a human and an animal. However, whether human or animal, the only reason for a living organism is as a vessel so it matters not how that vessel is created. There are some worlds where the whole of the population is engineered, no natural birth remains. These worlds are a hundred times more spiritually evolved than the human race. Engineering the vessels has, if anything, assisted with this, not hampered it.

CHAPTER NINE

MORE ABOUT THE SPIRIT WORLD

I return in this chapter, to pure teaching and philosophy about the nature of spirit. I regret, in Angela's phrase, "getting one's head around" some of the concepts is not a straightforward exercise!

Outside of the Collective, the Universal Spirit Council is the most important body of spirit, which is the topic I discuss first. It is to be distinguished from what has been referred to by others as The Council of Elders, which I describe next.

I then discuss the following questions:

- ❖ Is there specialisation in spirit?
- ❖ Are there soul study groups to look at lives that have taken place?
- ❖ What is the role of the Ring of Destiny in planning the next incarnation?
- ❖ Can one have a parallel life elsewhere?
- ❖ Does spirit have a concept of time?
- ❖ How is the future known before it happens?

My conclusion is entitled "Sense from it All" and "More Seriously". I then briefly discuss the planet's new spiritual cycle and its consequences for man.

UNIVERSAL SPIRIT COUNCIL

In book one, I gave a list of the things affected by spiritual level when in the spirit state. I promised to further elaborate on them in this, the next book. One of those things, membership of Council, I now describe.

Our guide related that this was going to be difficult for him to explain and for me to conceive, so he apologised in advance in case he repeated himself. He also apologised if he oversimplified the subject, as this would only be in an attempt to explain it as far as it is possible to do so. He asked me also to please be aware that we are not dealing with the physical body here, this is in no way similar to a human council where individual bodies gather and sit around a table to argue their opinions and attempt to persuade others to see matters from their point of view. In a human council such as this, it is necessary for the members to find words to explain their opinions, to produce evidence to substantiate their arguments. In the council of which he spoke, there is none of this.

WHAT IT IS

Council is a body of spirit. At this point the spirits concerned are still separate entities, but for attendance at Council, they are represented as one. I will further explain this; when a Three is to become a member of Council, the three individual spirits merge and are represented as one. This is because by the time they reach this stage, all their knowledge will be the same, they will have experienced together, either incarnated or by sharing on return to spirit, the same multitude of experiences and their acquired knowledge will be identical. Rather, therefore, than be represented as three with the same to offer, it is effective that they are represented as a one. This merging is only for Council however; at this stage they are still separate entities in all other matters.

Council is made up of many hundreds of these merged spirit entities and is one spirit body, one mass, as they all join together for the purpose. This means all joined members immediately know the combined acquired and experienced knowledge of all other members. In our terminology, a merging of minds perhaps? This is the greatest wealth of spiritual knowledge gathered together outside of the Collective itself.

WHAT IT DOES

We have spoken before of the fact that natural disasters are known in advance, that events of global proportion are known so that spirit Threes can script these events into the life-plans they make. Thus an earthquake, for instance, can offer many people a wide and varied range of experience, either as victim, survivor, bereaved, aid worker, reporter of the event, and so on. Spirit Threes will know that this is to occur and will be able to use it, if required, for these and many other reasons.

The task of the Council is to know all of these planetary occurrences for every planet in every solar system of every universe for the whole of time to come, and to make this knowledge available to all spirit Threes for their use. To do this they use the wealth of their combined experienced knowledge to date, to distribute with this planetary knowledge their advice on the experience that may be achieved by participation in the event. This is a very simplistic explanation of the unexplainable, I am afraid. Nothing is distributed, no flyers, no newspapers, no TV broadcasted news, nothing that relates in any way to our earthly means of passing information. To say that the spirit body, which is Council, just "thinks" it to all other spirit, is perhaps the nearest our guide could come to a description.

So, in summary, the task of Council is to know all planetary information to assist the Threes in the planning of their lives.

WHO QUALIFIES

In order to join Council, you must be either a Master, or in the final stages, six and seven, of level five. By this time you will have experienced sufficiently to offer the depth of knowledge required to be a useful addition to Council.

You are invited to join by Council, but it is not an invitation of the type that is refused, commanded rather than invited possibly comes closer. Not all Threes are requested to join, but this is a circumstance of numbers rather than ability. Council is required to be always at a certain mass. Threes will be leaving regularly when they decide the time is right to rejoin the Collective, and so others will be required to complete the mass.

It may be that a Three reaches the stage of readiness required for either joining the Council or Collective, but that there are no "vacancies" in Council so they return direct to the Collective. This does not signify that they are in any way less able that a Three that is invited to serve in Council, remember, there is no measure of superiority at all in spirit at any level, just time served. Membership of Council can be brief if a Three chooses soon to return to the Collective, or extended if the Three chooses to serve in this way for a length of time, the choice is made by the Three concerned. Having initially been co-opted into the Council, the choice is theirs as to how long they serve.

For those Threes who have not reached Master level yet, membership of Council is interspersed with incarnations, but on return to spirit they immediately return to Council. Their absence does not cause a drop in the level of the mass, only return to the Collective does this.

One last point as to the functions and powers of Council. Our guide believed he had described the function; the powers of the members are everything that it is possible for spirit to have and to do, although power is not a word he would choose to use. Power is an earthly concept; no such thing exists in spirit. The very concept of power indicates a superiority over others, the ability to have or to do that which others cannot and by this, exercise control or superiority. Power in this way does not exist in spirit. It is only a question of progression, of natural evolution. Membership of Council, however, requires that evolution to have reached or almost reached its end; requires that the spirit be as evolved as it is possible to be or in the final stages of that evolution, thus ensuring sufficient experience to carry out the work of Council and to add the appropriate level of usefulness to the mass.

We had an enquirer who had been told that in Spirit, he works with a higher group. It was called the Brethren of Christ, by the medium concerned. Our guide confirmed the enquirer, as a higher-level spirit, has been working for Council when in spirit and this is what the lady referred to. The medium herself was not fully aware of all the spiritual information that Angela and myself have been so privileged to receive, but was on the right track with her comment. The name is one used by those still struggling to fit spiritual information into the existing religious structure, rather than admit that the existing structure is incorrect. However, the group she referred to is the Council, who are indeed a group of higher-level beings.

COUNCIL OF ELDERS

The Council we have already mentioned is the "Universal Spirit Council", the very highest point of spiritual work before return to the Collective. As we have said, to work on this Council, all three must be in spirit as all three join together as one entity and in turn join as one body with the hundreds of other spirit entities doing this work although remaining as separate thirds for all other purposes. Their work is with planetary matters.

There is reference in some writings, to a Council of Elders, where newly returned souls are interviewed. This is not the Council to which I have just referred but something else.

Those serving on this council do so in their own account, as a one third, not by joining with their other two thirds. It is made up of level five spirit and Masters only, but is a much smaller council than the Universal Spirit Council. It is not necessary for all thirds to be returned to spirit in this case, although they usually are. The exception can be a third who has finished his incarnation but is awaiting the return of his other third who is still incarnated. An active guide with two incarnated thirds will not normally serve on this council.

The task of the council is the mandatory help with the review of the life for level one and two spirits, and the optional help by request for other levels, even fives and Masters if requested so to do (unusual but not unheard of). I would stress that this is not a judge and jury, no judgement is made, no punishment or retribution meted out, no praise or award given. It functions purely in an advisory capacity and to assist the soul concerned to form its own conclusion. Just as our guide does not tell me the answers till asked the questions so not to negate growth, neither would the council form judgement, which is the spirit's to form in order to obtain growth.

This raises the question, what is the reference to level of "teaching and guidance" in the context of the spirit levels? Our guide provided us with this clarification: *"All is known in spirit, there is nothing else to learn. However, it needs to be experienced. What the spiritual you does not have is the direct experience; there is nothing else it requires".*

If we may, let us return to the most useful analogy of a student about to embark on a study course. The student at the outset will be aware of the syllabus, the points that are to be covered. He will be provided with textbooks, which may well carry all the information he requires to gain or *experience* the knowledge required to pass his course.

If left to his own devices, however, he would possibly find it difficult to formulate and stick to a study plan; he may miss out certain important points and so have an incomplete knowledge of his subject. By having tutors or lecturers, he will be guided along his study path, given hints as to the content he should include, advised of his progress and where his weaknesses are. The onus will still be with him to do the work and undertake the study, but he will be greatly assisted by this extra input. (This is unlike a very young child starting out on a scholastic path, who will not have any knowledge to speak of and will require teaching at every step of the way).

So, our spirit starts its journey fully aware of the syllabus, knowing all that there is to know in spirit and needing to experience it all. In my first book I revealed that level one spirit has the life-plan written for it, level two has it written but with an eye to the spirit's own wishes, level three writes its own but has it checked and approved and so on. By "teaching and guidance" our guide referred to those spirit levels who do this writing and checking of plans. Depending on one's own level one may be found doing any of these things, to help lower level spirit achieve their life-plans with their incarnations and so gain spiritual evolution.

The other part of this is the assisting of lower level threes to assimilate the information and experiences gained on return to spirit. No judgement, no marks, just pass or fail, and a discussion to determine that they have indeed learned the lessons intended by the experiences of the lifetime. Not teaching exactly, but similar, and here the word is used in the context of abilities in spirit.

SPECIALISATION IN SPIRIT

We have a friend, who asked, "When we are all returned to spirit, are we all studying for a particular task?"

Our guide responded, *"In one sense, the answer should be no, you are all on the same path, spiritual advancement towards your ultimate goal of rejoining the Collective and this is the same path for every single spirit. However, spirit can specialise in a particular means of achieving its growth and the three of you here, together with the others of your group, all gravitate towards lives, which include planetary welfare and the care of your race. True, you have lived other lives on the road to this point, but many of these included a tendency to these pursuits within them."*

To clarify this answer, it was addressed to Angela, the enquirer and myself, hence "the three of you here".

Learning in spirit is not necessary, spirit just is! Nothing different is required of one spirit to another. All strive for the same goal; the experiencing of a syllabus of events that will teach ultimately about unconditional love. Tasks may befall certain spirit Threes on this journey, membership of Council for instance, but all will reach the same point eventually and rejoin the Collective.

SOUL STUDY GROUPS

There are soul study groups in which past lives are re-created and the impact of alternative choices played out. On return to spirit, the Three review the life, assimilate the information and experiences gained with the information and experiences gained from previous incarnations and decide where the life was successful or otherwise. In the case of level one and two this is done with input from others. All other levels do it within their Three, but may have outside input if they so wish it, even at level five stage as I have related previously.

At this point it is possible to watch your life played out, in order to correctly learn the lesson, identify success and failure, decide what needs replaying in future incarnations and so on. It is possible to change the moves and see what the outcome would have been if a different path had been followed.

Angela has read a reference in *"Conversations with God"* book three, to your life being like a game on a compact disc, which has every available ending programmed in and will produce an ending based on the moves selected during the game. This is a very accurate description, but then it would be considering its source!

The game is not released until such time as you return with your other third to spirit. It is then available for you to use and experience with the benefit of the life behind you, the different endings you could have achieved, good and bad, if you had made different choices. This is always done within a Three, but it may be that as higher level spirit, you are tasked with or wish to aid others in their progression by allowing what you call a "study group" to be formed and use a particular life game to illustrate a particularly valuable point.

This is done in the Library of Knowledge, and is the place where all of the "compact discs" will be stored until such time as you rejoin the Collective and take them with you. You choose whether a particular "disc" is to be part of the lending library and be used to assist others on their own journey, or whether it is to be in the archives, stored only, not available to others. Your choice, always your choice. No growth is gained or hampered by the choice of this; it is just a matter of preference at the time.

RING OF DESTINY

Reference has been made by one writer to a place of future life selection *"seen as a sphere containing highly concentrated force fields of glowing energy screens"* called the Ring of Destiny. This is correct; futuristic scenes of events and people the soul will encounter in a life to come are displayed there. Shakespeare's *Macbeth* contains many subtle spiritual references. The images of the future shown to Macbeth by the three witches, is a reference to the Ring of Destiny.

The Ring of Destiny is also called the "Room of Destiny" by some or simply "The Room". When a Three plan their life to come, they build in a variety of situations where choices may be made. The incarnated reaction to these situations determines the soul's achievement, or otherwise, of both the major and minor plots of that life.

In order to check that the plan they have devised is going to provide the necessary opportunities to achieve the desired lessons, they may take it to The Room and use the energy screens to play it through, making the choices first one way and then the other, to check that the life-plan works, that there are no errors in the programming to use the computer game analogy again. They can only do this for the forthcoming incarnation, not for ones in the future.

One thing that is a little misrepresented in the text I have been reading is the point it makes that only choices up to a certain point may be revealed to the soul so not to influence freewill choice. This is not correct. As the soul looses all memory on incarnation, freewill choice would not be influenced in this way. Our guide felt that what this refers to is the fact that the soul is not given direction in this room. It is not told that this is the correct choice and that is not. In this way, the outcome of the life is withheld. I think this has been slightly misinterpreted and shown as a refusal to show the choices past a certain point.

Once having determined that the plan holds sufficient choices, having built in some repeat chances for the more important aspects, should the original ones fail, checked it through for programming fault, to continue the analogy of the computer game, the soul can then incarnate and leave the maintenance and upgrading of the programme to its guide. This is what I have referred to in my books as re-scripting. When, despite the original planning, the soul makes unforeseen choices or errors, uses up all its chances to achieve a major plot or important sub-plot without getting it right, the spirit guide may step in to "upgrade the programme".

At that point, the guide may write in new characters and new parts to the plot. The guide can also use The Room to check the plan and see the result should one or the other choice be made. Remember déjà vu, The Room provides another aspect to it, a feeling of been here, done this, seen this, heard this, can be a reference to a vague and distant memory of playing your own life through before incarnation.

SPIRIT AND TIME

It is not possible to have a parallel life elsewhere, contrary to some science fictions. The reasons are, first, on Earth, we have a concept of time. Things change, evolve, live, die. In our world, because of this, it would not be possible to have two incarnations or more happening at once. The theory that all time is happening together, just in different dimensions, does not work on Earth. If the year 1800 happened in a different dimension to the year 2001, how would you know the history of it in 2001? If 10th March 2001 were to happen in a different dimension to 9th March 2001, there would be no tomorrow. A simplistic approach to a favourite science fiction topic of man, but enough to serve as an indication of the point. So, on Earth or indeed on any other planet, all time is not happening at once and all lives are not lived at the same time.

Point two is that time is different in other worlds. Spirit still incarnates, stays for a span of time and leaves, but the structure of time is completely different in nearly every world.

Point three, and the one which has become confused in some philosophies, giving rise to this concept of all things happening at once, is the nature of time spent in spirit. When you incarnate on Earth and spend, let us say eighty of your years there, it is only as if you have been gone from spirit for a few moments. It is one beat of the spiritual heart, one drawn breath. This is the same whether you incarnate for eighty years or eight minutes! No difference in spirit. This is why incarnations over thousands of Earth years are possible; it is only thousands of years in Earthly terms, spirit has no concept relating to thousands of years.

Spirit is a dimension rather than a place, there is no planet called "spirit", no world, it is a dimensional realm we occupy when not incarnated. Again, our guide advised, this is something we as a race do not have the understanding for, such understanding will come with the planet's evolution, but not yet for some time.

You will hear it said, "There is no time in spirit". This is correct, in the spiritual dimension there is no time as we know it. Spirit entities split from the Collective, work through their journey and associated spirit based activities and then rejoin the Collective, with nothing to measure the time this takes.

As there is no time to measure the journey by, it is therefore true to say that in spirit terms, all is now. There is no yesterday and no tomorrow. All **is** now. This in turn has given rise to the belief that lives can exist at the same time in other parallels. In spirit terms, if all is now, then all lives must be occurring now, but in the terms of the actual worlds where the incarnations take place, time exists and as time exists, there is tomorrow and yesterday and so multiple lives cannot occur together.

To further complicate it, although all is now in spirit, spirit only deals with one incarnation at any one point in the now. How could two incarnate and one remain behind if all lives were simultaneous? Our guide said he realised again, this is a huge over simplification if we employ our world's science fiction ideas to it, but in truth, it is simple. We deal with one incarnation at once, and we deal with one between incarnation return to spirit at once, but each one we deal with is *the now*. We know of all the others, but only those that have occurred. We do not have the experiences of the lives yet to be lived until they have been, but when they have, they become *the now*.

There is an order of progression to spirit as we know, stages and levels, councils and teachings, but our guide concluded, spirit does not have time by which to measure progression. In spirit this is a most natural state, just as the passing of time is natural to our world.

THE FUTURE KNOWN

This would seem an appropriate point to revisit this topic, which I raised in my first book. The future is known, all major events on all planets are known, all wars are known, all disasters are known, all major accidents are known, all of man's destinies are known, our guide related.

Subject of course to freewill choice, but that too is known to a degree, but only whilst in spirit of course, because of amnesia on incarnation. What is not known are the events that can be attributed only to the daily act of living. For instance, you may walk out of your front door and trip, but catch yourself and no more will be thought of it or occur from it. That is the product of daily living. Again, you may walk out of the door, trip and fall, causing a head injury, subsequent disability and trauma to yourself and those around you, loss of lifestyle, loss of income, loss of self-esteem, loss of mobility. This most assuredly would be a known event. I think this successfully illustrates the difference.

Let us think of a life-plan. When you plan your life prior to incarnation, you plan the major plot, the major sub-plots and the minor sub-plots. You write in the circumstances that you think will provide these lessons, you select parents, you know who your major players are going to be to a great degree, often selected from within your soul collection as we call it.

True, if you make freewill choices that take you away from your plan, your guide will script in new scenarios and people to try and bring things back on track, but in the main, when you are ready to incarnate you know in broad terms how this life is going to run, know what is in store, know the plot, know the future! You may not know that you will have a head cold on 2nd February 2004, or that you will trap your finger in the door on 5th June 2006, but you will know the broad outline of the events that are due to take place in your life to enable you to achieve your plan for the life.

Our guide urged us to take that framework and apply it to planets. This time, instead of a spirit entity, a part of a Three making the plan for the life to come, we have the Collective Consciousness making the plan for the universe, indeed, for all of existence. The plan was made in broad terms for every single planet so that spirit entities would be able to enjoy a rich and varied collection of experiences on their spiritual journey and so that the Collective itself would be enriched by this on the eventual return of each Three. Again, this plan is in broad terms and just as freewill choice can hamper a life-plan, so can the intervention of life forms hamper a planetary plan. Just as a spirit guide can re-script to give his thirds a second chance, even a third, fourth or subsequent chances, so can the Council arrange matters at planetary level.

Our guide asked me to remember his teachings about Council; that the task of the Council is to know all planetary occurrences for every planet in every solar system of every universe for the whole of time to come and to make this knowledge available to all spirit Threes for their use. Council knows of these events because they are in the plan made by the Collective Consciousness before the physical dimension started.

So, in summary, before the commencement of the physical dimension, the Collective designed a plan for it in a similar way to a spirit Three designing a plan for a forthcoming incarnation. Spirit Threes know the future of their forthcoming incarnation, subject to freewill choice and the freewill choice of others. In the same way the future of the physical dimension is known, subject to the interference of life forms and their freewill choices. (But, of course, these freewill choices and interferences are known, too).

So I conclude that writing an individual life-plan is more a series of choices than starting with a bare canvas. The life-plan is more like choosing the colours of a tapestry already drawn, the tapestry being the known future of a civilisation, its culture, science and technology.

As I have said earlier in this chapter, but I think it is a point worth repeating, in spirit all futures of all worlds in all dimensions are known. Wars, natural disasters, unnatural disasters, discoveries, explorations, advances in science and technology, cultural fashions and achievements, all these are known. When forming a life-plan, a spirit Three has available to them all of these choices in which to set their play and with which to provide the necessary lessons they require from the plan. So, to continue my analogy, you not only choose the colours of a tapestry already drawn, but also choose which part of it you wish to stitch in this life.

The reason the future is known is because the Collective is "Editor in Chief". We humans are "the journalists" who write our individual stories, providing the details and "bringing to life" the events, but the broadsheet is under the control of an Editor, who knows the future content.

So how does a spirit Three know the future? The Collective knows all, knows every future event. In spirit, you too know all that is to happen, by the spiritual ability to attune with the Collective and "know what it knows". A little like a journalist doing his research at the library before writing his headlines. It is from this "research" that you write your plan and it is up to your guide and the other guides to act as sub-editors to see that every opportunity is afforded to you to complete the script once your have taken incarnation.

THE SYLLABUS

The Collective before the commencement of the physical dimension determined the stages and levels in spirit. *"Conversations with God"* comes close to an explanation, when it talks of the Collective needing to know itself and doing this by the experiences of incarnated spirits. When it decided on this as a means to know itself, and to be enriched so to continue, it designed the cycle of splitting, journeying and returning. It also established the framework for the journey and established the dimension and framework for the in-between state, which we refer to as spirit.

As the physical dimension evolved, so did the spiritual one, continued our guide. Eventually it became as intended by the Collective. It mirrored the framework of the original blueprint and has been this way since that time. Our guide is of course talking of many millions of our years, but as we now know, the spiritual dimension has no measure of time in the way that we do. This is a difficult concept for those within an earthly incarnation to understand. The spiritual part of us already knows all of what our guide is saying. It is my task in my earthly incarnated state, to try and understand it in this lifetime and relay it to you, my reader!

SENSE FROM IT ALL?

With the book's numerous examples, I trust I have convinced the reader that *"All the world's a stage",* that we write our own scripts (or have them written for us). Included therein will be choice of props, the key fellow actors, the major plot and the sub-plots, all designed to help us experience love in its many aspects, both positive and negative. As for the setting and grand events, these are not our decision, so our individual script can seem like a dot on a picture composed of millions of dots that is already composed and drawn, and which is ever changing according to a pre-made plan.

Unlike a public play however, there are no rehearsals, except you must try again if you make a total mess of it. Worse than that, although you knew the script when you set out for the theatre, you suffer amnesia just before you arrive! So, too, does the rest of the cast and the audience!

The only saving grace is the prompt, the spirit guide. He knows the storyline and can give you assistance. The problem is, his prompting is not obvious at times, but he does ensure as far as he is able, that you meet your fellow actors at the right time and that the stage props are in place.

Now, in case this is all too easy, the script contains critical options in places. Here the actor must make a decision, which is either the correct or incorrect choice, without any help from the prompt.

To perform the play once might be sufficient fun, but because the message in the play is about a complex subject, love, we perform hundreds of times in many different theatres! You may at times wonder, "What the hell is going on?" People may be firing live rounds at you, you become seriously ill, the cashier runs off with the box office receipts and you don't get paid. The script contains many snakes and ladders.

Young actors may cry "foul", and in the extreme, walk off stage; older hands usually play to the end but even they slip up at times. You do get feedback for each performance, not from the audience, but you become your own critic along with your two soul-mates, as you review your own show each time after it's over. You also get to review your soul-mate's show and have a hand in their next script.

The reward for all this is that we rise up the spiritual ladder eventually to achieve master status and then go home to God, our point of origin. All this is based on His original idea. He also supplied the physical world in which it takes place. Earth is one of the theatres, and this is why we return to human form.

MORE SERIOUSLY

Life is a crossword puzzle. Socrates famously remarked, *"The unexamined life is not worth living!"* The challenge of finding our true spiritual nature is indeed a large one. Not everyone will go on a spiritual quest, only a minority. Even for those that do, a wake-up call in the form of personal trauma is often necessary.

The spiritual journey for all is the acquiring of unconditional love. This is not a reference to love as we know it in the physical, but the state of the soul when in spirit; pure and unconditional. It is the aim of all to reach this state whilst in the incarnated form. This is not achieved until one reaches the stage of true spiritual master on the earth plane, but may be strived towards in each incarnation. Being aware of the reason for existence is a huge step in one's growth and sharing one's gifts unconditionally with others is the next.

Socrates also said, *"To find yourself, think for yourself"*. But, of course, we need tools to think with and we need to conquer existing prejudices and conditioning before we arrive at new concepts, or, as I would prefer to say, before we recognise what we already know at the level of the soul. Reincarnation and life-plans are the conceptual navigational aids to finding ourselves.

Past lives are a major clue to solving the crossword puzzle of life. It is regrettable that past lives are only on the margins of recognition (or at least that is my experience). The media does now have occasional references to the topic. We have found that once the subject is raised, there are a surprising number of people who can accept the phenomenon, but who normally would shy away from the topic for fear of being thought strange or eccentric. Those that have the conviction may need to take heart sometimes, from the life of Gandhi. When asked how he found the resolve to struggle alone for human rights, he replied, *"Even as a minority of one, the truth will always be the truth."*

A more recent thinker than Socrates has a profound line, *"To see your drama clearly is to be liberated from it"* (Ken Keyes Jr). Much easier said than done, but my earnest wish is that this book has been a help to the reader in seeing their own life more clearly. The summary of the spiritual reasoning behind my own past lives that I gave at the beginning of chapter three, plus the extracts from mediumship that made up chapter eight, I trust have helped the reader to see life's drama more clearly. The meaning of life is not to be found in a calculation of personal monetary worth, nor in conspicuous consumption, but in our experiences. Unfortunately most likely in those experiences that are the least comfortable and least easily endured.

WHAT NEXT?

The year 2000 marked the start of a new, higher spiritual cycle for the planet. Amongst other things, there are being born more and more children with past life memories. In time, they and many others will hopefully "find their way" to books such as this one and know, not only are those memories true, but also come to understand the spiritual perspective for life. They will hopefully go on to achieve their destiny. In many cases, this will be similar to my own, helping to raise spiritual awareness, to bring others to the knowledge they will have reached and to achieve their wish earnestly to share this with others.

At the present time, there are children who are choosing to incarnate on to the planet, who have an advanced degree of spirituality. Many are returning, bringing with them their accrued knowledge from previous lives and with an inbuilt knowledge of their own spirituality. Unfortunately, mainstream education, the medical profession and in some cases, parents themselves are unaware of this and do not know how to nurture and assist these children. They are being labelled Attention Deficit Disorder (ADD) or ADHD by the "system". They may alternatively be labelled "Autistic", again incorrectly. These children have a spiritual destiny, to assist the raising of the spiritual vibration on the planet. The condition has now been noted by eminent practitioners, and has been termed "Indigo", derived from the colour of their auras, which are completely indigo blue, the spiritual colour.

The spirit council members responsible for overseeing Earth have said the planet experiences 2000-year cycles and that one has just ended and a new one begun. In addition, Earth is undergoing a period of catch up both in technology and spiritually, which has been taking place for approximately the last hundred years to have it "on pace" for the start of this new cycle.

They have further said that it is intended within this particular new cycle that Earth reaches the point of no longer being a nursery world, and elevates to the next level, but in order to do this, it is necessary for the populace to reach a higher spiritual consciousness. By that they do not mean that the whole world will become as spiritually aware as those incarnated older ones, who currently work for spirit, but certainly that the inhabitants should raise their consciousness sufficiently to allow this to occur.

Angela and I were told on the evening before the September 11th tragedy in New York, that disasters, both man made and natural, would get worse in order to get better. This is one of the first of these man made disasters so predicted. What will occur from this is further atrocity, further sacrifice of the innocent and a coming to the brink for mankind. What will follow is a universal condemnation of such acts, leading to a universal lift in spiritual consciousness. The first step on the ladder of progression, and a very large one.

During this period, more and more people will feel abhorrence at what is occurring and seek the spiritual path. More and more will turn from what has become normal to them in search of what must surely be better, realising that normal does not signify as what should be, just as what is accepted!

The council members have revealed that mankind is in urgent need of being able to raise his vibration, to use his intelligence to understand the need to progress emotionally and spiritually, and not just technically. Man has been slow to take the step of spiritual progression that is now required, so that Earth may become a planet of higher spiritual consciousness and leave behind the low stature of nursery world, so that another world can take its place in that role.

They continued by saying that as man became "civilised", he began to interfere with the natural order of things, with the planet's natural energies, so that these are now damaged. The consequences of this have led to more wars, atrocities, acts of needless violence, famine, drought and natural disaster. The topic of natural earth energies, what these are and how they can be used for personal and for planetary healing, will be the major topic of my next book

APPENDIX ONE

MORE ABOUT ANIMAL SPIRITS

In *"Why Come Back?"* I discussed animal spirit reincarnating here and on other worlds, just as we do. We have had more than one enquirer who wished to know whether animals reincarnate to the same owner in this life or from previous lives. The clue to this can be the new pet adopting the same habits as a deceased one and having an instant familiarity with its surroundings.

Our guide confirmed that pets can, but do not always reincarnate to the same owner and that animals from past incarnations may, too, incarnate to you in this one. He gave us an illustration, which came as an initial surprise to us.

At the time, a neighbour's cat was a frequent visitor to our house. We described him as having "an attitude problem", so strongly did he communicate his wishes to us. He would visit our home and quite simply take over, as if it was his right to do so! He would sit in front of the fridge for example making it quite clear that he expected to be fed, and then be quite particular in his food.

Our guide advised that the cat had belonged to the two of us in more than one shared incarnation and that he had been my cat alone in yet another. Out of pure curiosity, we asked the cat's spiritual age and were completely amazed at the answer of two thousand, five hundred years, give or take a few. He is nearing the end of his journey. His age is nothing in comparison to our own spiritual ages, but for an animal spirit, is quite advanced. Their paths are shorter as they have far fewer lessons to learn, and do not have the range of emotions and experiences to work through as does the spirit that incarnates as human.

One of our friends recognised in her current pet spaniel, the same spirit as that of the pet spaniel she had twenty-three years earlier (Both happen to be spaniels in this instance, but they do not necessarily reincarnate as the same breed, or indeed, even the same species). Her guide further advised this was the same dog and what is more, was the reincarnation of a dog from a past life. In the previous incarnation she and the dog had been close, as she had taken comfort from the little dog in the absence of much other love in that life.

So how do pets interact with life-plans? Do we choose pets, do pets choose us? Do they plan their lives as we do, or are they planned for them? We choose pets in the main, before incarnation. There are occasions, of course, when a pet is scripted in by the spirit third to fulfil some plot thrown up by the life that is unfolding.

The pets themselves have their lives determined for them in spirit, but follow the same route of progression by the learning of spiritual love. They, of course, usually respond to love with a simplicity not often found in humans. It is no accident that they often incarnate to the same masters as in the case of our friend's dog, or find their way to the master to experience what it is necessary for them to experience for their own growth. It is just an extension of plans interacting with each other.

Many pet owners have had to face that difficult decision of either ending a pet's life or letting a terminal illness take its course. We have a friend whose pet horse had begun to suffer illness in old age. She took the heart-rending decision to end his life. She asked her guide if he could give her any information about her pet, now he was in spirit.

He responded that he was concerned for our friend at this emotional time; that he tried to help make the transition easy for both her and her horse. He went on to confirm the horse is now returned to his spirit state and so will not suffer as he would have done if he had continued to live. Our friend had made exactly the right decision. He went on to confirm that she had shared a previous life with the horse, and that the horse had itself experienced two other incarnations as a horse, and many lives as other animals.

As previously related, a soul that can incarnate on Earth as a human, cannot come back in the future as an animal, any more that a cat can incarnate as a man. A cat can incarnate as a dog or other animal of the same classification, but even though we are mammals, too, we are set apart by our degree of intelligence and ability to talk etc.

Animals and all living organisms carry their own type of spirit and reincarnate as other animals, fish, birds and so on. We also related that they do not choose their own path. Instead it is arranged for them by the Collective and may be scripted in to interact with human lives as part of the various plans. The animal, however, will have no choice in that. It would have perhaps been more accurate to say that the plan is arranged for the animal by spirit entities charged with this work by the Collective, but it amounts to the same thing really as all spirit is part of the Collective collecting experience for it as we know.

I wrote in *"Why Come Back?"* the concept of the Three does not apply to animals in the same way as it does to humans. Instead they form a spirit mass and these masses are divided with the divisions being designated to incarnate as the various classifications, animals, birds, plants and so on.

What it appears that I did not make clear in my first book, is that at this point, when the mass has so divided and a portion has been designated to be, for instance animals, it is then divided further into smaller particles which we will term individual spirit particles. Each of these particles then divides into three, in the same way as a human spirit entity does, and one part of the three remains behind while the other two incarnate. They will both incarnate as the same type of animal, for instance, they will both be dogs or both be cats. The difference is that the incarnated two thirds may not ever meet or interact with each other.

It is not required at this level of evolution that this should be the case as their meeting could have little impact on their eventual life experience, well at least, certainly not in the way that it does for humans and other races of the same degree of evolution or greater. The one remaining behind is a guide to the other two, but again, in a most limited way, because the plans do not have the degree of complexity that our own do. The master spirit who designed the plan will also oversee the guide; he will not be left alone to oversee the incarnations.

The two incarnated ones will lead completely separate lives in most cases and as each one returns to spirit, it will join the remaining third immediately so that the third becomes two thirds and then on the arrival of the last third, it is immediately a complete entity ready for a master to direct into further incarnations.

As we said, each incarnating third will incarnate as the same type of animal; for instance both will be dogs, but one may be a Spaniel and one an Alsatian. The remaining third has no recognisable form, it is just spirit. The law about appearing in the guise of the last shared incarnation does not operate here. Human thirds (or I should say, the spirit that can be human because this relates to all incarnations of this type of spirit, not just earthly ones), retain their individuality (unless summoned to serve on council) as separate thirds until their eventual return to the Collective. Animal spirit and the spirit of all other life forms, become one entity again after each incarnation and then split anew for the next, so do not retain individual identity.

When I have confirmed to enquirers that a dog owned now is a dog owned previously, it would be more accurate to say that the dog owned now is from the same spirit entity as the dog owned previously as the spirit regroups and re-divides each time. This may be difficult for some to grasp, so it is simpler and not untrue to confirm it as the same dog.

Dogs may be lions next or cats but will hold their classification. Mammals will be mammals, reptiles will be reptiles, birds will be birds and so on, until rejoining the Collective and leaving again in a different spirit mass. At all times the mass is being replenished by spirit leaving the Collective to experience incarnations. At the same time it is being reduced by spirit rejoining the Collective and so enriching it in its own way, with the fruit of its experiences. The major difference is that this is all controlled by the Collective or indeed, the spirit entities charged with the task on behalf of the Collective.

It is also true that most birds and mammals have spiritual contact with their remaining third as a natural matter of course. Fish and reptiles do not, nor do insects and plant life. Mammals however have sufficient intelligence and communication skill to have such a contact without having evolved sufficiently to lose it as so many of our own race have!

In the first book I mentioned animals that seem to exude an almost human intelligence. I said that these are the older, many times incarnated ones that are almost ready to return to the Collective. This is quite true, I just failed to make clear the point about becoming one and re-dividing each time before these incarnations. It is also true that many animals have awareness of the spiritual presence of a "human" spirit in addition to their own ability to have spiritual contact with their own guide as we will term their remaining spiritual third, but again only the more evolved spiritually. It is also true that these animals may well be drawn to higher spiritual humans as they feel with their unique sense, the spiritual closeness between them.

In a nutshell, animal entities do divide into three with a guide remaining behind, but the guide does not have the degree of importance it has when one reaches the level of human and other species of that classification in other worlds. This is when the laws and rules of spirit governing the interaction of Threes begins and becomes important. Prior to this it is just "the way of it", a thing that happens but not of real importance. The guide is just a part of the entity acting as an anchor or base for the other two to home in on when they return and a point of spiritual communication should they need it for direction while incarnated. They do not interact with their other third while incarnated as we do, and do not retain identity between incarnations.

Having gone into this amount of detail about animals, the vegetarians may well further decry the carnivores among us. We have been asked if vegetarianism is necessary in order to be spiritual. Our guide responded, *"No, most assuredly not. There are planets where it is the norm, but it is not the case on Earth. Vegetarianism is something that should be viewed in its relation to the world in which you are incarnated. It is a physical matter, not a spiritual one. Animals that incarnate on Earth are quite likely to form part of the food chain; it is a physical effect of incarnation on Earth for them. It is not incorrect for humans as the higher species, to use them for food, as this is the way of it on Earth. If a human chooses not to do so and to be vegetarian, that is a freewill choice or it may be a life-plan choice, but it is not in everyone's plan to do this, nor should meat eaters feel any guilt for choosing to eat meat."* I would miss bacon sandwiches if I had to give up meat, so that's a relief!

APPENDIX TWO

DEALING WITH SCEPTICISM

I would hope this heading is not necessary, but I am aware those not fully accepting of spirit may read the book. Of those that do find their way to it, many may have a partner who does not have the same degree of acceptance and so I include it as it may help. However, the basic fact is that the coming to the realisation of spirit and spiritual truths is for the individual to discover for himself if it is to signify spiritual growth whilst incarnated.

I wish merely to share my knowledge with anyone whose degree of curiosity about the world is similar to how mine once was. The scientists may well retort, "Unsubstantiated metaphysical thought"! As I concluded in my first book, life is not what it seems. There is another reality, another dimension, outside of our daily awareness, but the fact we are mostly unaware of it does not deny its existence. "We don't know what we don't know" has been often said. Unless you can cross the secular / spiritual divide with open-mindedness and accept that statement, we do not have a mutual starting point.

Scepticism is disbelief. An exercise for the sceptic might be to set out reasons why he or she disbelieves and what they disbelieve. Then to draw up a list of what can be accepted. Given open-mindedness and especially given contact with spiritual people, it may well be found that one list shrinks whilst the other grows.

Knowing that I do not carry out whatever instructed to do in books, I have compiled my own list, which I attach. This list is biased of course. The reader only has my word for it when I say I am not the same person in my thoughts and beliefs that I was in my twenties and thirties. I would have then had both feet firmly in the scientific camp! The test is to find spirit unaided by seeing through the false clues and perhaps taking some wrong turnings before making the right ones.

The spiritual truths are there for the grasping, but it takes effort to secure them. It is as if they are on the tip of the tongue, or in a recess of the mind just beyond the power of recall. Just as electricity makes a spark when it jumps an air gap, so for us to make the connection we must use the power of imagination to make the leap across the gap. To quote an unknown philosopher, *"Man cannot discover new oceans until he has courage to lose sight of the shore"*.

It would not be advantageous to try and persuade one who is not "ready" of the validity of the spiritual teachings we (and others) have received. Spirits that have journeyed and "graduated" through sufficient levels to be able to accept our writings will be greatly aided by them; will view them as the missing pieces to a puzzle that has occupied their life so far. There is always a certain recognition of the "truth within it", when the person is ready. To try to force the issue in one not ready will be fruitless for all concerned.

For a hardened sceptic, no amount of argument or persuasion will dent the armour. Sadly the Dalai Lama was correct in his observation *"Suffering is often the catalyst to the spiritual quest"*. Paradoxically, a lifetime without trauma is likely to be the least conducive to spiritual search.

We would like spirit to give us amazing proof positive of the way of it, but this would not be advantageous for us. Part of spiritual growth is to come to an understanding, to be able to "see" the way of it for oneself, while in the incarnated state. This is the task; this is the "exam" for entry to the next class.

A person in the media eye that I admire for the public way he has chosen to show his spiritual growth in his lifetime, is the "disgraced" former banker and politician, Jonathan Aitken. Here is a man, who was once chairman of a bank, had the prestige, possessions and lifestyle of such a position. He entered politics and became a junior minister. A gilded life one might think. Then to quote his writings, *"It was the journey through the dire straits that started my searchings. Mine were direr than most, for in the space of two years, I experienced the public agonies of defeat, disgrace, divorce, bankruptcy and gaol"*. He went on to study theology for two years and acquired a faith *"in an apparently absent and unanswering God"*. To me, what a hero! Unfortunately, to most of the rest of the world, what a fool!

There are those in the incarnated state with no remembrance of their spiritual identity at all. There are those who are fully accepting and then there are those who have the interest, who are desperate to follow and believe, but have the doubt within themselves. The guides tell us if they were to give proof positive, where would be the progression? What would the person have achieved? It would be like sitting an exam with the answer paper in front of you. It would be like attempting a crossword puzzle and being given the answers with each clue; there would be no effort or struggle involved, no sense of achievement or pride in accomplishment. Sometimes I wish my own "clues" had not been so emotionally painful!

The double-whammy of divorce and bereavement, for me personally, were the life events that offered me the opportunity ultimately of taking the conceptual leap to realise I am a spiritual being having an earthly experience. It can sometimes happen as in my own case, that it is only in later life that one finds the belief and trust in spirit that one may desperately seek.

For those struggling to accept, the spiritual advice of what to do for their inner peace and growth is to cease to search for proof. Accept what you can at this time, meet those who "fall" into your way, talk with others of an advanced spiritual nature and gradually absorb spiritual information. The real task is to listen to those with the rational explanation for everything, but still be able to form one's own opinion in the face of such rationality.

For those who have doubts but want to believe, it may well be that at the moment, it is not spirit's intention to bring the person to full acceptance in this lifetime; they may not be ready for this. It may be intended to raise the questions that will allow them to understand their doubt and accept it as part of the progressive path, rather than as a negative thing that they should seek to suppress. In due course they may realise why it is not correct for them or anyone else to receive proof positive, unless they have first achieved complete acceptance on their own.

So, how did that happen in my own case? My early search included reading with great interest accounts of near death experiences (NDE). There is a whole world of difference, though, between reading and experiencing. I have not personally had a

NDE, but Angela, my partner has. Someone once told me about their past lives, but I could not accept the phenomenon at the time, and dismissed them as crazy. It was not until I had my own past life regression and had images from two of my past lives appear, that I received my evidence and so became convinced about reincarnation. This was some years later, when I was on a spiritual quest.

Perhaps some of the most persuasive evidence is personally being able to benefit from spiritual healing in one or more of its many applications. There is a catch twenty-two here, as without spiritual beliefs, one may not attempt to use it. To have the remedy, for it to work effectively, one must have the belief; one must validate the treatment. Benefiting from spiritual healing or from past life therapy is the nearest one can perhaps come to proof positive. I have related how Angela now leads a fairly normal life, not without some pain, whereas she was told she would be disabled for life.

Before leaving this topic, there is a gender bias to be considered. I noticed, as you may have, that those attending spiritualist church, mediums themselves and those seeking mediumship, are in the majority, female. I asked our guide why this was so. There are two spiritual explanations for this, the first concerns ease of raising vibrational level and the second concerning spirit level.

The vibrational level in the female human is easier to lift than in the male. To reach spiritual awareness, the male must work harder. This is why, when returning as a level five spirit, most will take at least one male incarnation for the greater challenge. Added to this is the fact that level five spirit, both male and female, are likely to publicise their spirituality; they are more comfortable with it and have the spiritual maturity to cope with it, to not be afraid of it.

Of course, level five spirit is in a minority on Earth. Level one spirits who form the majority, have greater difficulty in displaying any degree of spirituality that they may achieve. Of these, the female, having the lighter vibration, has less trouble with allowing this to be openly seen by others. This is why the majority of the participants in spiritual groups are female; the majority of those who seek mediumship are female and so on.

The male at that level may have an interest, but will not wish to show it. He will find some difficulty in rising above his inbred embarrassment and need to appear in the eyes of others, as the strong, red-blooded male. The male level one spirit, will find many of the spiritual concepts emasculating in the human form. It goes without saying that this only occurs in the Earthly form and is an added challenge to incarnation, concluded our guide.

WHY ON EARTH ACCEPT SPIRIT?

FOR	AGAINST
1. The voice in the medium's head that tells me accurate facts about my life, points to a reality outside my daily awareness.	A voice in the head is the classic symptom of schizophrenia.
2. The breathtaking complexity of the human body, and indeed of all life, points to the fact that there must be a "Maker", a Higher Power.	Life on Earth arose spontaneously, a combination of the necessary ingredients and a long period of time.
3. Messages from a loved one received through a medium point to continuation of consciousness after so-called death.	Gimmickry and guesswork. Death is finality.
4. Certain current life likes and phobias, health issues not subject to a conventional diagnosis, can be explained by past lives.	Unsubstantiated metaphysics.
5. Images obtained during a past life regression confirm the feeling of having lived before, or explain an attachment to an era	The product of an overactive imagination.

in history.

6. Spiritual healing brings cure, or at least alleviates symptoms without drugs.	Spontaneous remission.
7. Some ancient civilisations show evidence of an advanced knowledge of architecture, mathematics and astronomy, quite out of keeping with the general level of development and indicating knowledge "imported" to earth.	Science is still working on its explanation.
8. Consciousness would not have come into existence merely to disappear at the end of a single lifetime.	You only live once; life is not a rehearsal. Death is the end.
9. Suffering has an ulterior purpose. Changes can be seen in some people who have grown spiritually through their experiences.	Life's a bitch and then you die!
10. Joy often arises from helping others; material goods produce short-lived satisfaction only.	He who dies with most toys, wins. I consume, therefore I am.
11. Differences in reaction between people in response to the same event is caused by differences in their spirituality and spiritual level.	Nature or nurture or a combination thereof, determines behaviour.
12. Differences between siblings in their character traits, eg intelligence, philanthropy, empathy has spiritual level as its primary cause.	Genetics account for the differences in siblings.

13. Unconditional love is the greatest force to bring about change for the better in people and the world.

Weapons and armies are.

14. The results obtainable by visualisation indicate powers of the human mind not yet generally accessed, and are further evidence of a reality outside our daily awareness.

Only that which is within the current scientific framework can be accepted.

15. Thoughts that jump into one's mind seemingly from nowhere, is evidence of spirit communication.

The brain is a complex organ. The subconscious mind throws up thoughts randomly.

16. Telepathy between two people is evidence of a spiritual connection and possibly of past lives together.

Science is still working on an explanation.

17. A spirit can materialise and appear as "mist" or have an historical appearance. Sometimes these can be captured in photographs.

Photographs can be faked. Natural phenomenon can explain so-called ghosts!

18. A psychic artist of no previous acquaintance can draw from spirit a portrait that has an uncanny resemblance to a person in a family photograph album (because the one is the spirit of the other).

Coincidence.

19. Inner peace comes from recognising and following a destiny (or life path).

Power and wealth create security.

20. Personal growth comes from experiencing love in all its

How I am feeling now is as good as it gets. Growth is not

aspects; you are complete when you can let everything be.	attainable, an invention of the psychobabble industry.
21. Identical twin studies have shown that where separated into different families, major life events have been remarkably similar, showing life-plan at work.	Identical twins separated at birth with the same life events have genetic predisposition for explanation.

This is my list. I know which I prefer, but then I am a reformed character who has "served his time" throughout many past lives.

BIBLIOGRAPHY

This book is based on questions and answers with our joint spirit guide, whom I introduced as Tjelamunra in my first book, as that is how he appears to Angela, who is my communication link to him. Although there are no books on which this one is based, I have referred in passing to other works and these I now list.

Introduction

Neale Donald Walsch "Conversations With God, Book One", Hodder and Stoughton, 1997

Roger J Burman "Why Come Back?", Quiet Waters Publishing, 2002

Sylvia Brown "Past Lives, Future Healing", Judy Piatkus, 2001

Chapter Three

Richard Hough "Captain James Cook, a Biography", Hodder and Stoughton, 1994

Alistair Maclean "Captain Cook", William Collins Sons, 1972, Book Club Associates Edition, 1974. (The portrait of Furneaux is on page 105 and that of Omai by Joshua Reynolds in on page 129.)

Chapter Four

John Keegan "The First World War", Random House UK, 1998

Chapter Seven

Hazel Courtney "Divine Intervention", Cico Books

Marie Louise Lacey "Know Yourself Through Colour", Aquarian

Chapter Eight

Brian Weiss "Through Time Into Healing", Judy Piatkus, 1998

Chapter Nine

Neale Donald Walsch "Conversations With God, Book Three", Hodder and Stoughton, 1998.

ABOUT THE AUTHOR

Upon meeting a new partner in January 2000 (the timing no accident), Roger Burman has found his spiritual abilities have really accelerated. He has found through his partner Angela, that he can access the equivalent of a "Cosmic Encyclopaedia". Any question he could ask, provided it was not of a directly personal bent, has been answered by spirit; the answer being sometimes a few lines, sometimes pages.

Roger asked the questions that have always dogged him – the meaning of life, why people behave as they do, why life is so painful at times.

Having previously discovered reincarnation, Roger's next question was why. Hence the title of the book, "Why Come Back?" in which he puts into narrative form the many questions he put to spirit and the answers he received.

Until his spiritual awakening, Roger had a conventional life of marriage, children, a professional occupation and a university degree. Quite normal, until that is, at age forty-eight, he was told by spirit, *"You are going to write a book."*

His expertise or authority to do this is no different to any other persons, as we are all spiritual beings. We are all equal and have full knowledge when in our natural spirit state. The difference is only one of ability to have spirit communication at a time when spirit is wishing to impart new knowledge.

The recognition of his destiny and the life-changing experience of receiving the spiritual teachings, has given rise to Roger selling his business and home. He now offers workshops and forums for spiritual matters on board his converted Scottish fishing boat, 'Quiet Waters'.